T

Dominican Republic

REG BUTLER

In Association with
THOMSON HOLIDAYS

1994

SETTLE PRESS

While every reasonable care has been taken by the author and publisher in presenting the information in this book, no responsibility can be taken by them or by Thomson Holidays for any inaccuracies. Information and prices were correct at time of printing.

Text © 1993 Reg Butler

All rights reserved. No part of this publication may be reproduced or transmitted in any form or by any means without permission.
First published by Settle Press
10 Boyne Terrace Mews
London W11 3LR

ISBN (Paperback) 1 872876 12 9
ISBN (Hardback) 1 872876 11 0

Printed by Villiers Publications
19 Sylvan Avenue
London N3 2LE
Cover by Thumb Design Partnership
Maps by Mary Butler

Foreword

As Britain's leading holiday company operating to the Caribbean, Thomson are happy to be associated with Reg Butler's new book 'The Key to the Dominican Republic'. In writing the book, the author worked closely with our resident representatives who have year-round contact with holidaymakers' travel interests.

Whether you have chosen to stay on the Amber Coast or in one of the south coast resorts, we feel this pocket book can act as a quick reference guide to the sightseeing potential beyond the beaches.

It's impossible to see everything in one or two weeks. When the holiday is over, we suggest you keep this guidebook to help plan your return visit – perhaps to the other coast which you didn't have time to explore.

All prices mentioned in the text were accurate at the time of printing. But the Dominican Republic has an inflation problem, and local prices will certainly change during the coming year. However, any costs quoted in the book can serve as guidance to the average level of expenses.

THOMSON HOLIDAYS   1994

Contents

		Page
1.	**DISCOVER THE DOMINICAN REPUBLIC**	7

2. PLANNING TO GO
2.1	Which season? Monthly min/max temperatures	11
2.2	Visa and entry regulations	13
2.3	Changing money; credit cards; regulations	13
2.4	What to pack, and what to wear	14
2.5	Health and medicine	14

3. THE AMBER COAST
3.1	Introduction	17
3.2	Arrival – orientation	18
3.3	Puerto Plata	18
3.4	Playa Dorada	20
3.5	Sosúa	22
3.6	Costambar; Cofresi	24
3.7	Take a trip	
	East along the coast	26
	West along the coast	30
	Inland to Santiago	31
3.8	Nightlife – Casinos, discos	33

4. SANTO DOMINGO
4.1	Introduction to Santo Domingo	35
4.2	Arrival & Hotels	36
4.3	The Colonial Zone	
	4.3.1 Santo Domingo Cathedral	37
	4.3.2 Ozama Fortress	38
	4.3.3 Calle Las Damas	38
	4.3.4 Columbus Alcazar	40
	4.3.5 Tostado House; St Francis Monastery	40
4.4	Other sights and museums in Santo Domingo	
	4.4.1 Columbus Lighthouse, Three Eyes, Aquarium	41
	4.4.2 Plaza de la Cultura; Museum of Dominican Man and other museums	42
4.5	Shopping – El Conde Street; Avenida Mella	42
	Duty Free	43
4.6	Nightlife – casinos and discos	43

5. THE SOUTH COAST
5.1	Introduction to the Caribbean coast	44
5.2	Orientation	45
5.3	The resorts	
	Boca Chica	45
	Juan Dolio	47
	Casa de Campo	48
	Punta Caña	49
5.4	Take a trip	49
5.5	Shopping	51
5.6	Nightlife	51

6. DOMINICAN REPUBLIC BEYOND THE BEACHES
6.1 Basic geography ... 52
6.2 The historical background ... 53
6.3 The economy ... 56
6.4 Cash crops and fruit ... 57

7. SHOPPING ... 60
Business hours – where and what to buy

8. EATING AND DRINKING ... 62

9. TRANSPORT ... 65
Transport – taxis, moto-conchos, long-distance bus, car and motor-cycle rental

10. LEARN SOME SPANISH ... 68

11. TRAVEL TIPS AND INFORMATION
11.1 Entertainment ... 71
11.2 Sports ... 73
11.3 Tipping ... 74
11.4 Electricity ... 74
11.5 Dominicana time ... 74
11.6 Phoning home ... 75
11.7 Newspapers, radio & TV ... 75
11.8 Security ... 76
11.9 Photo hints ... 76

12. FURTHER REFERENCE
12.1 Quick facts ... 78
12.2 Festivals and public holidays ... 79
12.3 Useful addresses ... 80

Maps

The Caribbean Islands ... 8
The Dominican Republic ... 10
Playa Dorada ... 21
The Amber Coast ... 27
Santo Domingo – Colonial Zone ... 39

Chapter One

Discover The Dominican Republic

From 1492 the Spaniards came looking for gold, and sent expeditions into the interior. But in 1974 the Central Bank of the Dominican Republic recognised that 20th-century goldmines were sandy beaches. Protecting the country's golden-sand reserves, the Central Bank bought up long stretches of coastline. The financial acumen paid off. Investors arrived, world-class golf courses were built, and development was launched of luxurious hotel resorts. The process continues.

Today the Playa Dorada – Spanish for Golden Beach – is among the prime destinations of the two million annual visitors to the island republic. Still more beaches are opening up, along the southern and eastern coasts.

Even though Columbus came in 1492, the island has only in recent years been 'discovered' by international beach-lovers and sun-worshippers.

What to expect, apart from the usual tropical paradise of blue sea, golden sand and coconut trees?

Firstly, the background culture is Spanish: Latin American music, afternoon siestas, very late nightlife, and a laid-back confidence that problems will be solved *mañana*.

To highlight the Spanish heritage, the tourism ministry is now trying to promote the country's name as Dominicana – a shortened version of its official Spanish name of la República Dominicana – rather than the English-sounding Dominican Republic. This may cause confusion with the former British colony of Dominica, which is no relation. But that confusion already exists, with the two islands regularly receiving each other's mail.

The language and culture of the Dominican Republic date from the discovery of the country by Columbus, with the capital – Santo Domingo – established as the oldest Spanish city in the Western Hemisphere. Spanish rule lasted for over 300 years.

As a late arrival on the tourism scene, the Dominican Republic has learned from other nations. There is a total ban on the high-rise Miami look. Developments are married into the landscape. With over ten percent of the country designated as National Parks or Scientific

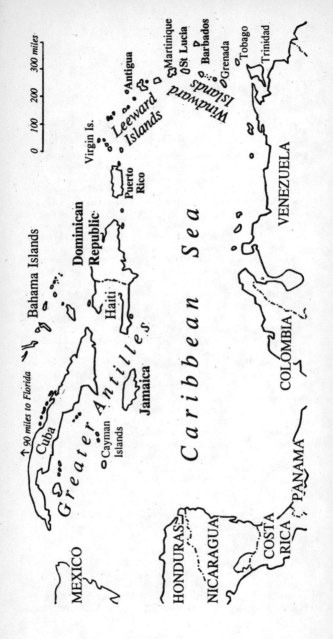

Reserves, there is good protection for the environment and for endangered species.

In this third world country, tourism is welcomed with a big smile. Typically, in a land of frequent electric power failures, the tourist areas are 'spoilt' by having absolute priority in keeping the current flowing. Nobody wants to irritate the nation's biggest source of hard-currency earnings.

Most of the resorts are purpose built for an international clientele. Especially popular is the all-inclusive 'club' concept of hotel-resort operation. A high proportion of resort accommodation is available only on a full board basis, with use of sport equipment and live entertainment as part of the holiday package.

Even drinks can be included, though usually limited to 'national' drinks only – beer, house wine and any cocktail based on rum. Imported drinks are excluded, because of the very high import duties.

Most visitors come mainly for the beaches, watersports and nightlife of the principal resorts. For the sport-minded, there's every available facility from tennis to volleyball, ping-pong and golf.

But much of the Dominican Republic's special magic lies beyond the resorts. The terrain is rugged, with alternating bands of mountain ranges, valleys and plains. More than a third of the total area lies above 1,500 ft. There are mountain retreats that are sometimes called the Alps of the Caribbean, with the highest peak soaring to 10,562 ft.

The country offers fantastic scenic diversity from cacti to rain forests, mangrove lagoons to cascading waterfalls in the mountains. Sheltered coves and river inlets were greatly favoured by pirate vessels that laid in wait for treasure-laden Spanish galleons.

Whether your choice is northern coast or southern, there is potential to reach closer to the lifestyle of the Dominican Republic. Everywhere there are friendly faces. Music and dance have an enormous influence on Dominican life. In streets, restaurants and bars there is a permanent flow of music, recorded or live. The national dance is merengue, backed by every variation from the Caribbean and Latin America.

The 1992 celebrations to mark the fifth centenary of the Columbus voyages have awakened interest in he Dominican Republic's share in that history. Much of the story can be followed in the Colonial Zone of Santo Domingo, where the Columbus family was deeply involved for at least seventy epoch-making years.

Christopher Columbus himself loved the island, which he described as the most beautiful in the world. Like Columbus, you will probably want to make return journeys, to discover more about this fascinating holiday destination.

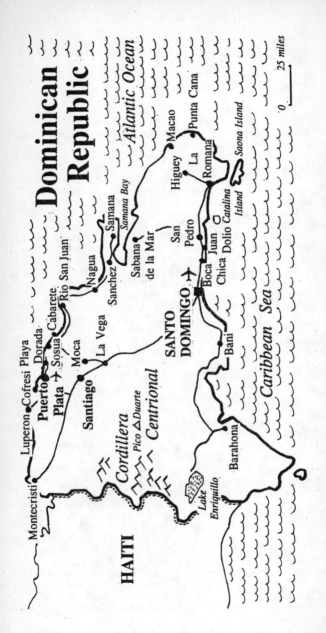

Chapter Two

Planning to go

2.1 Which season?

In coastal areas you can expect a warm tropical climate with a year-round average of 25 degrees C – around 77 F. August is the warmest month, January the coolest. But really the difference is not significant, ranging from 73 degrees in winter to 82 degrees in summer. Trade winds keep the air cool and fresh.

A milder climate typifies the central region. In the Highlands, temperatures can drop 30 degrees especially around the 10,417-ft Duarte Peak. December to April temperatures can even dip below freezing on mountain heights.

A local tourist publication puts forward its weather prediction:

> Today – sunshine
> Mañana – sunshine
> Two weeks ago – sunshine
> For the next 14 days – sunshine.

In truth, rain is not unknown, and the northern coast collects around 60 inches a year. The rainfalls are typically tropical – in buckets, but of short duration. They come mainly during afternoon or evening and bring a slight drop in temperature. After daytime rains, the sun rapidly reappears and everything soon dries out. The rain may be heavy, but need not wreck your day.

Because of the central mountain chain, the south gets less rainfall. The southwestern provinces of Azua, Barahona and Pedernales comprise the country's driest region, with cactus near the Haitian border.

June through November is the prime season for Caribbean hurricanes. But most of them by-pass the Dominican Republic. Anyway, resort hotels are solidly built to cope.

TEMPERATURES — Average daily maximum and minimum temperatures — °F.
RAINFALL — Average monthly precipitation in inches.

	J	F	M	A	M	J	J	A	S	O	N	D	Annual rainfall
PUERTO PLATA													
Max	81	81	82	84	84	88	88	88	88	88	84	82	
Min	66	64	66	68	70	72	73	73	72	72	70	66	
Rain	2.4	1.0	2.0	3.9	6.7	5.9	5.9	5.9	7.1	5.9	4.7	2.4	53.8"
SANTO DOMINGO													
Max	84	84	84	86	86	88	88	88	88	88	86	84	
Min	66	66	68	70	72	73	73	73	73	72	70	68	
Rain	2.0	1.7	1.7	2.7	7.4	6.0	7.0	6.2	6.5	6.7	3.8	2.8	54.4"
JUAN DOLIO													
Max	84	84	86	88	88	88	88	90	90	88	88	86	
Min	66	66	68	70	72	73	73	73	73	72	70	68	
Rain	1.1	1.1	1.0	2.2	5.0	3.9	4.2	4.5	5.7	5.7	3.9	1.6	39.9"
PUNTA CANA													
Max	81	81	82	82	86	86	86	88	88	86	86	82	
Min	72	72	72	73	75	75	75	77	77	75	75	73	
Rain	2.4	1.8	2.0	2.3	4.3	4.3	3.1	3.8	3.5	5.3	4.6	3.1	40.6"

2.2 Visa and Entry formalities

No visas are needed for holders of British, US, Canadian and most other European passports, which should be valid for six months after your planned date of return. A return or onward ticket is required.

Foreign visitors must purchase a US$ 10.00 tourist card and pay a US$ 10.00 departure tax on departure. Tour operators such as Thomson Holidays include these charges in the cost of the holiday package.

Before landing, passengers are given an immigration form to fill out. The immigration official gives it a quick glance, and you're through. Luggage trolleys are available as far as the customs desks. If required, porters are available for assistance with luggage thereafter.

At the exit you are met by tour reps who escort you to the minibus for transfer to your hotel. Minibuses are small in the Dominican Republic, and luggage space is limited. So luggage usually goes into a separate vehicle. Visitors travelling independently will hopefully find taxis awaiting at the airport.

2.3 Money

The Dominican peso is written as RD$. It is illegal to take pesos in or out of the country. The exchange rate has been pegged at RD$ 12.50 = US$ 1.00. That rate is liable to change, in line with inflation.

Notes come in denominations of 5, 10, 20, 50, 100, 500 and 1,000. They are all the same size, but vary in colour. There are coins, but you're likely to see only the one-peso piece. Shops normally round up to the nearest peso, ignoring the fact of centavos.

Depending on the cross-rate between dollars and sterling, the pound was theoretically trading at around RD$ 18 – roughly 5p to the peso. In practice, you'll always get the best rate with US dollars, and it's advisable to travel with US dollar travellers' cheques and banknotes, rather than sterling or any other hard currency.

Currency must be changed into Dominican Pesos at airport booths, exchange bureaux at major hotels or at commercial banks. Airport change offices are open from 9-15 hrs. Banking hours are 8.30 to 15.30 hrs Monday-Friday, while some banks also open Saturdays in the main towns. Bureaux at hotels often stay open until 20 hrs.

Your passport is required for cashing traveller cheques and also for getting cash on credit cards. Warning: a charge of 5% or 6% is made on *all* credit card transactions. That applies to any purchases made with plastic, where the price is loaded by that percentage. But no charge is made for changing cash or traveller cheques.

All exchange outside of banks and official bureaux is totally illegal. Any street deal can leave you shortchanged by light-fingered operators.

Departure
Keep your bank slip when changing money, as this is needed for any final re-conversion of remaining pesos into dollars, or possibly sterling if they have any in stock. You can reconvert a maximum of 30% of the total bank receipts produced. That transaction can be done only at the airport on departure. But sometimes there's a long queue and general chaos; or the exchange clerks extend their lunchhour, especially on those exhausting days when maybe six or more charters are arriving and departing within a few hectic hours. Aim to spend up your pesos, just keeping some in reserve for a final drink at the airport.

2.4 What to wear and pack

The Dominican Republic can be hot and humid, so beach and lightweight casual clothing is the order of the day. Topless is OK around hotel pools, and on beaches which are not easily accessible to local Dominicans. Shorts and sleeveless shirts are not permitted in landmark churches, casinos and some restaurants.

Evenings tend to be smarter, but still casual. Sport jackets and cocktail attire are recommended for elegant evenings out. Take a lightweight sweater for the chill of air-conditioned restaurants.

Laundry service is available in some hotels. Simply leave a message for the maid and allow 24/48 hours for laundering. You can expect to pay £3 for a dress and £2 for a shirt.

Pack any personal equipment you may need for sport activities, such as tennis racket, snorkelling gear, or a helmet if you intend to rent a scooter. Throughout the summer, unexpected downpours of rain can be very refreshing. However, you may find an umbrella useful.

Don't forget to pack your favourite suntan lotion, toiletries and any medicines which you take regularly. Insect repellents can be a blessing.

2.5 Health precautions

Jabs
No vaccination certificates are required. Some medical people lean heavily towards ultra-caution, and recommend a full range of inoculations against Typhoid, Polio, Tetanus and Hepatitis A. Others suggest that these precautions are not essential if you are taking normal care of yourself, and not visiting any outlandish areas. The Caribbean islands are rated as a low-risk area. However, ask your own doctor's advice at least four weeks before departure. For further details on health requirements contact the Hospital for Tropical Diseases Healthline on 0839 337 722. Code number 23.

Mosquitoes
Have your defences ready against mosquitoes, which come in 57 varieties. Mosquitoes bite especially at dusk when they are hungry for supper. They are very partial to holiday-makers. It's wise to be frugal in use of perfumes and aftershaves, as these seem to attract them. Insect repellents are sold at chemists and in hotel-resort shops.

An excellent mosquito deterrent is (believe-it-or-not) Avon's "Skin-so-soft" bath oil spray. It's highly effective. Even sand-flies will keep their distance.

For a peaceful night's sleep, keep your windows closed after dark, and have any mosquito screens in place. Leave the air conditioner switched on.

There is no malaria risk in the resort areas. But if you intend to spend time in Haiti or near the Haitian border, anti-malaria tablets should be taken during the week before travel.

Sun and health
Deep suntan is often regarded as a sign of health, but doctors advise caution against overdoing it, because of skin-cancer risk. To avoid sunburn, the standard advice is well enough known. But many holidaymakers don't fully realise the power of the tropical sun, which can still burn even if you are sitting in the shade, where bright sunshine can be reflected off water or sand. Ultraviolet rays can also strike through clouds, though a heavy overcast sky does offer some protection.

When working on your sun tan, go easy for the first few days. Take the sun in very small doses and wear a wide-brimmed sun hat, or a baseball-type cap. Take extra care whenever your shadow is shorter than your height. The shorter your shadow, the more risk of sunburn. Avoid the UV danger time between noon and 2 p.m. Resume your sunbathing late afternoon when the sun is not so strong.

Use plenty of high-factor suntan lotion – SPF of 15 or over – reapplied every hour or so after you've been in the pool. Wear a T-shirt while swimming or snorkelling. If your exposed skin has turned pink or red by evening, be more careful next day!

Hopefully you'll go home with a tan that's golden and not lobster red or peeling. Be cautious about beachside hair-braiding services which expose strips of your scalp to the sun. Wear a head covering. It's no fun to get a sunburnt scalp.

In case of heatstroke – marked by headache, flushed skin and high temperature – get medical advice. Meanwhile wrap yourself in wet towels, and drink fruit juice or water.

Finally, beware of iced drinks while sunbathing, and then jumping in the pool. Your tummy is bound to rebel.

Water

Take seriously the warnings about not drinking tap water. In the Dominican Republic, piped water standards are not so high as in Europe or North America. The only dependable source is water that has been 'purified', or which comes from a natural spring source in the mountains.

There's nothing to worry about in the principal hotels and restaurants, which use only purified water for drinks and ice cubes. But in down-market bars and restaurants be leery of ice cubes which could be frozen tap water. A clue is that factory-supplied purified ice has a small hole in it. If you're doubtful, fish out the ice cubes, or finish the drink before the ice has melted.

Some hotels keep your room supplied with bottled water, and have an ice-making machine down the corridor. Otherwise, if you find it's costing you two dollars for a tiny bottle of water from the mini-bar, buy a gallon container far cheaper from a supermarket. If you're going out for the day, it may be worth taking a small supply with you.

Stomach upsets

Most upsets are caused by unaccustomed food, very cold drinks and hot sun. If you're not accustomed to quantities of fresh fruit, go easy at first with all that tempting tropical produce. Give your stomach time to attune itself to a deluge of pineapple juice, piña coladas, and banana mamas. Be wary about down-market local restaurants, where kitchen standards may be less than ideal.

If you want to come prepared, bring pharmaceuticals such as Lomotil, Imodium or Arrêt, which are usually effective. Imodium can be bought at any UK chemists. Usually the problem takes 24 hours to clear up. If your stomach is still complaining after a couple of days, go to see the doctor. There's no point in suffering. He'll fix you with tablets or an injection.

Chapter Three

The Amber Coast

3.1 Introduction

Named the Amber Coast for its abundance of amber deposits, the northern shore of Hispaniola is where Columbus landed in 1492. The first Spanish settlers came looking for gold, but were disappointed in their dreams of a quick fortune. During the 16th century, the numerous natural coves and river inlets became havens for buccaneers and pirates, who found a quicker way to a golden harvest, lying in wait for treasure-laden Spanish galleons.

In late 20th century, the Dominican Republic has begun developing a more reliable income from the region's 75 miles of white and golden sands. There are coastal lagoons with brilliant clear waters, set against a backdrop of lush green mountains. Government tourist policy has aimed at developing selected areas of the coastline, which is served mainly by charter flights into Puerto Plata airport. Within a short distance is the Playa Dorada vacation complex, just east of Puerto Plata city. Hotel and 'club' resorts are centred around an 18-hole golf course designed by Robert Trent Jones. Landscape gardeners have transformed the entire zone into a purpose-built holiday getaway.

The complex is the first of several which are planned to spring up along the Amber Coast within the next few years - especially in the area of Sosúa and Cabarete, and at Playa Grande further east.

Each hotel or club features its distinctive style of amenities and dining options, land and water sports. The all-inclusive concept is popular in many establishments, even to the provision of unlimited local drinks throughout the day. Water sport devotees have every facility for water-skiing, sailing, wind-surfing and scuba-diving.

Arrangements vary. Some hotels offer one hour free every day for wind-surfing, snorkelling and sail-boating. Any other sports like banana boat, scuba-diving and water-skiing, you pay direct at the water-sport centre. Prices are often listed in US dollars, but you can pay in pesos. There is insurance cover on all these sports.

From breakfast till past midnight there is choice of full programmes of other in-house sport activities and entertainment. But even along the developed shoreline of Playa Dorada, there are still plentiful beach areas where a visitor can enjoy total tranquility. Other guests may prefer to work on their suntan around the pool, keeping thirst at bay with an exotic rum punch.

With virtually everything provided, many visitors are reluctant to stir past their club entrance gate. But outside is the workaday Dominican Republic, which also has its fascination. It's a pity to come so far, without getting closer to the Caribbean experience. From the Playa Dorada enclave, it's only 10 or 15 minutes by bus or taxi into Puerto Plata city; or, in the other direction, to the Mediterranean-style resort of Sosúa.

On a smaller scale, the same can be said of hotel developments at Cofresí or Costambar, west of Puerto Plata. In those two locations, resort development has gone hand-in-hand with the building of upmarket villas and apartments, designed specially for foreigners who want a holiday or retirement home in the tropical sun.

With a hired vehicle or on a sightseeing tour by minibus or boat, it's easy to explore deserted beaches and sparkling bays, backed by a dense growth of coconut palms and other tropical trees.

Further afield, it's worth visiting the major cities of Santiago or Santo Domingo on day trips. Travelling across the island, today's explorer passes through a landscape which Christopher Columbus described as "the most beautiful country which has ever been seen by human eyes." See it for yourself!

3.2 Arrival & orientation

Most visitors to the Amber coast arrive by charter airline at Puerto Plata airport, which has recently been expanded to cope with the fast-growing number of visitors. Outside the terminal, you'll soon get your first view of Caribbean vegetation, with palm trees rustling in the breeze. Green plantations remind you that Hispaniola is an island of sugar.

Driving past a typical village, you'll also get your first culture-shock reminder that the Dominican Republic is a third world country, poor by Western standards. But, because of the lush fertility of the island, nobody goes hungry.

The main highway goes east to Sosúa and Cabarete; west to Playa Dorada, Puerto Plata, Costambar and Cofresí.

3.3 Puerto Plata

Puerto Plata is the name for the city of 85,000 population, and also for the province which includes virtually

every developed beach along the northern c
name, meaning 'Port of Silver', was given by Christopher Columbus in 1493, when he was attracted by the shimmering waters of Puerto Plata bay. His brother Bartholomew founded the town in 1496.

The city's development quickened in 1504 by order of the island governor Nicolas de Ovando, who wanted to expand the harbour facilities. At first the town prospered, but then went into decline as Spain became more interested in richer lands. As protection against French and English pirates, the fortress of San Felipe was built in 1540.

Meanwhile, the residents turned to contraband trading, to the irritation of the Spanish Crown. Finally the destruction of Puerto Plata was ordered by royal decree, and the citizens were relocated to the southern coast. Even so, bootlegging flourished into the 17th century.

In 1742 came the re-birth of Puerto Plata, with an influx of settlers from the Canary Islands. Since then, the city has become one of the country's leading urban centres, especially as the main outlet for the interior's export products such as coffee, cocoa beans and tobacco. Part of the population depends on fishing.

In the Industrial Free Zone they make T-shirts, gin, mink coats and international-label shirts. Otherwise, the most important cash crop is the tourism of Puerta Plata province, based on the miles of beaches: Luperón, Cofresí, Costambar, Long Beach, Playa Dorada and through to Sosúa and Cabarete.

The backdrop to Puerto Plata is **Mount Isabel de Torres**, reaching an altitude of 2,565 feet and accessible by Italian-built cable car – a ten-minute ride, if it's operational. The limestone peak is protected as a Scientific Reserve under the National Parks administration. Characteristic plants around the hilltop botanical park are Sierra Palm, Wild Tamarind and Satinleaf. On lower slopes is Dominican Mahogany.

Dominating the crest is a huge statue of Christ the Redeemer, overlooking spectacular vistas. At the statue's base is a crafts centre, selling local products.

The main historic site of Puerto Plata is **San Felipe Fortress** – the only remaining structure from the original settlement, with ancient cannons' commanding the harbour.

Visitors can inspect the modest museum, and the cell in which the national hero, Juan Pablo Duarte, was held prisoner in 1844. The fortress was also used as a prison during the time of Dictator Trujillo. Near the fort is a monument to General Luperón, another national hero who came to power in 1879.

The central focus of the city is **Independence Park**, with the twin-towered Church of San Felipe alongside, acting as a landmark. An essential visit is to the **Amber**

Museum close by, where the upper floor is devoted entirely to the gem-stone. The lower floor is equally dedicated to souvenirs.

In this area of Puerto Plata are many wooden houses in 19th century style. They give an impression of how the town looked towards the end of colonial times. It's interesting just to drift around casually, absorbing the Caribbean life-style.

There is a street called 'Separacion' which separated the rich areas from the poor. The waterfront promenade, called the **Malecon**, is extremely wide with very little traffic. There are some quite elegant villas, and apartment developments. But other streets lead into a hinterland of run-down property.

Several hotels are grouped near Long Beach, including the **Puerto Plata Beach Resort**, which faces the sea shore. Its casino is a lively evening centre. The town has a number of good restaurants. But they find it hard to survive when so many of the resort hotels feature full board.

Part of the regular sightseeing circuit is a visit to the **Brugal** factory where rum is aged and bottled – a daily output of 9,000 cases of 24 bottles each. The distillation process is carried on elsewhere. After a taster, it's worth buying at prices that are remarkably cheap. Whatever the age and quality of rum that you choose, the cost is less than in any retail outlet.

3.4 Playa Dorada

Just about every leisure and sport activity is featured in this prime resort of the Dominican Republic. Wrapped around the central golf course, each of the very spacious first-class hotel resorts has its own entrance gate with round-the-clock guards to ensure that only authorised persons gain admission.

All guests at the all-inclusive clubs wear a coloured plastic bracelet or a locket to identify their right to freely-provided meals, drinks and use of facilities. For admission to the Paradise Club, for instance, your ID is a yellow wrist-band.

Each hotel tends the beach which is part of its frontage, fully equipped with every facility for sun-bathing and water-sports. The beach itself is public, though casual access is not easy for non-residents at any of the hotels. At weekends, however, there is some influx of residents from neighbouring Puerto Plata. Otherwise a holidaymaker could spend an entire vacation without seeing anyone who's not a hotel servant or beach attendant.

Every establishment is brilliant with tropical flowers, and shaded with flamboyant trees and shrubs. In the Jack Tar Village all the main shrubs and trees are labelled with their Latin name. There is nothing to disturb the eye.

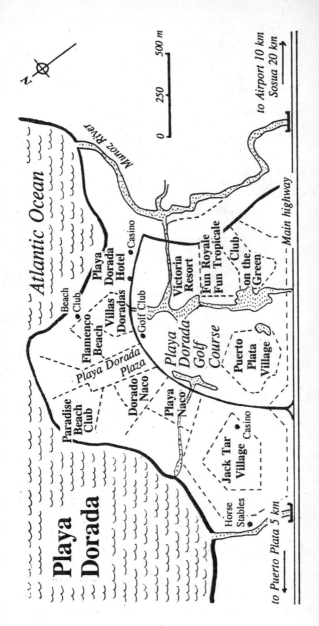

A full range of holiday shopping can be done without venturing past the outer boundaries of Playa Dorada. Each hotel has a minimarket, and there are tented souvenir bazaars on the beach, operated by authorised vendors. The central Plaza has a shopping mall, a bank, Harrison's the jewellers, and Hemingways restaurant for cheeseburgers and French fries.

'Sleeping policemen' ensure that motor traffic cannot move much faster than the ponderous push-bikes or tandems available free or for a small charge. Bike trails provide interesting circuits within the perimeter of Playa Dorada.

Horse-riding is a popular option, along the beach or up into the lush green mountains in the background. Within Playa Dorada is the beachside Rancho Gran Chaparral, run by the company that operates the golf course, and located within walking distance of Jack Tar Village. From other hotels, riders are fetched by horse-carriage.

All-day tours costing about US $42 are guided through tropical forest, beside banana plantations and sugar cane fields and across rivers. There are many opportunities for taking pictures of country cabins built from palm wood and thatched with palm leaves.

Occasional halts are made: at a village bar; beside a mountain stream for a dip; and at a small restaurant for a buffet lunch of rice and beans with fried chicken and pork, yucca and other local vegetables. Finally it's back to the ranch, to end with a brisk 10-minute gallop up and down the beach – because, by that time, everyone is familiar with his horse.

The chosen route may also pass by a Haitian village. Numbers of Haitians are permanently settled in the area, used as seasonal cheap labour for cutting of sugar cane. There is great contrast between Dominican and Haitian villages. Most Dominican houses have at least a concrete base, and proper walls. But the Haitian shacks are much more rickety, with a roof which is not always waterproof.

By all means enjoy the very Americanized, ultra-clean and ultra-safe environment of Playa Dorada. But it represents only one aspect of the Caribbean. One way or another, it's worth enlarging your experience of the island by seeing first-hand the other sides of Dominican life.

If you don't want to travel by horse, bicycle, rented vehicle, public transport or tour bus, every hotel displays a fixed-price list of taxi fares to standard destinations: about £5 to Puerto Plata; £7 to or from Costambar; £10 to Sosúa.

3.5 Sosúa

Located 15 miles east of Puerto Plata, Sosúa has grown from the influx in 1940 of German and Austrian Jewish refugees. Shortly before World War 11, President Trujillo had offered a haven to Jewish emigrants. Land was allocated at Sosúa, and 500 families arrived. Among them were doctors, lawyers and teachers. Initially they were housed in buildings left by a fruit-packing company which had pulled out earlier in the century.

The district was called El Batey. That name was given in Spanish colonial days to slave quarters, which were normally set up downwind from the plantation owner's mansion. The word is still applied to the temporary living quarters for itinerant cane cutters.

Among their activities, the Jewish community set up a dairy cooperative and a sausage factory, based on cattle ranching in the region. These enterprises still operate, making Sosúa the cheese and salami capital of the Amber Coast. But the settlers were more accustomed to big-city life, and mostly they moved on to USA soon after the war ended.

Today, what little remains of that settlement is well integrated, so that few traces remain. But a hotel or two is Jewish owned, a small synagogue holds occasional services, and typical street names are Calle David Stern and Calle Dr. Rosen.

Meanwhile, tourism has totally transformed Sosúa, wrapped around its fabulous local beaches. The El Batey district has gone up-market, with building of air-conditioned international hotels and dozens of restaurants from fast-food to gourmet.

The main street called Calle Pedro Clisante is lined with travel agencies, bike-rental dealers, souvenir stores, boutiques, art galleries, supermarkets, bars and discos.

The longest stretch of utterly perfect sand is the main Sosúa Beach, but there are several smaller beaches such as Puerto Chiquito, Playa Chiquita and La Playita.

Typical is the idyllic little beach of La Playita: fine, golden sand with a semi-circle of rock to mark its boundaries. The background facilities form part of the Casa Marina Beach Club. No beach is private, but it feels that way.

Down the hill leading to Sosúa Beach is a fantastic array of colourful souvenir booths. Haggling is the name of the game. Nothing has a price tag. The market continues all along the main beach, where vendors display local products that range from Haitian-style paintings to wood-carvings, pottery and T-shirts. They can hire out beach chairs, braid your hair, or sell you oysters, coconuts or a bottle of rum.

Sosúa Beach itself is wide, with soft golden sand backed by tropical trees. Informal bars and restaurants are spread along the one-kilometre beach.

Halfway along is the Beach Boys bar, operated by Yorkshireman Mike Lambe, who used to manage pubs in Weatherby and Knaresborough. He proclaims 'Free Beer tomorrow' and is a great source of background information on what restaurants to visit, and where to go.

Worth trying is a coral-viewing cruise on a glass-bottomed boat, floating slowly over the reef which protects the bay. One of the boats has a French Canadian captain who knows his marine biology: naming the tropical fish and explaining their habitat. Price is around £5 for a one-hour trip.

Sosúa Beach splits the town into two distinct areas: the El Batey of international tourism, and Los Charamicos which is much less developed. It's a cheerful district of tin-roofed houses, with typically Dominican atmosphere, merengue music everywhere. Currently there are many changes, as bars, discos and restaurants are re-decorated under new management, to cater for Sosúa visitors who want to get closer to the local Dominican Republic life.

Sosúa is more Mediterranean in atmosphere than any other resort on the island. Happy Hours of 'two drinks for the price of one' put everyone in convivial mood. In the evening along the main streets, restaurant staff try to tempt you to dine with them, offering free drinks. It's all done in light-hearted friendly style – persistent but not aggressive. You can just refuse the offer by half-promising 'tomorrow'. Mañana can be a most useful word! You can eat well, at prices like £10 each for a meal with drinks and a rum nightcap.

On the tip of the bay, an oceanfront villa was formerly owned by the US Ambassador to the Dominican Republic. Today the villa has been converted into an Italian restaurant called La Puntilla de Pier Giorgio, offering a more glamorous mealtime experience. Customers are picked up by horse carriage. For reservations call 571-2215.

In a similar spectacular position, but nearer to Sosúa Beach, is El Coral Restaurant which also features dancing to a live band most evenings. Elsewhere is lively choice of bars, and nightclubs such as 'Barock' and 'Tropics'. Casino Playa Chiquita offers the usual gaming range from slots and Bingo to Blackjack and Stud Poker. Marien's night club rounds off the action.

3.6 West of Puerto Plata

Costambar

Located only three miles from downtown Puerto Plata, this hillside location has been developed with white and pastel-coloured villas and low-profile apartment blocks, mainly as a retirement haven for North Americans and Europeans. Pink and white are the dominant construction colours, each residence set amid lush gardens and well-manicured lawns.

Tranquility is the keynote. Sleeping policemen ensure that the occasional vehicle crawls around at a decorous pace. Even motor-bikes ridden by macho Dominicans are tamed.

A prime hilltop location is taken by the Bayside Hill Resort and Beach Club, which offers a birds'-eye view of the Isabel de Torres mountain and of Puerto Plata harbour. The hotel makes good use of split levels, with water cascades and swimming pools.

Free daily transport is offered to the centre of Puerto Plata, and also to the Dorado Naco beach resort in Playa Dorada. A minibus shuttles every 20 minutes to Costambar's own beach. The shore is only a few minutes' away, but the bus is most welcome for the steep return uphill. The sands are extremely wide and stretch for over a mile, with a colour range from off-white to golden.

The open beach and the 9-hole Los Mangos golf course serve the entire community of villa and hotel residents. There are other sport facilities such as tennis, but it's not really a location for dedicated water-sport fans. A day at Playa Dorada would be a better bet – accessible by a scheduled bus, or taxi.

Otherwise a plus point could be the almost total absence of beach vendors, apart from a small tented bazaar nearer to Club Isabella. A sunworshipper could spend all day without being approached by a postcard salesman. A thatched beach restaurant specialises in grilled lobster, shrimp kebabs and barbecued chicken at very reasonable prices.

Cofresí
Four miles west of Puerto Plata, Cofresí is a self-contained resort and residential community, somewhat like Costambar, with villas scattered down the hillside. An almost-circular bay encloses crystal clear waters with a half-mile shoreline shaded by coconut palms. There's a panoramic view round to Costambar in the next bay. The entire setting is natural, not built-up, ideal for escape in laid-back style, away from the hustle and bustle.

If you're tempted, building plots are offered for sale at $25 per square metre. A potential bonus is that, according to legend, pirate treasure is buried somewhere around. Indeed, Cofresí itself is named after a famous pirate.

Hotel Elisabeth offers good ocean views, and its Blue Marlin restaurant is recommended for grilled lobster. But the main development is the Cofresí Hotel & Club, which features all-inclusive holidays. Facilities and accommodation are terraced on different levels of the hillside. Palm trees are everywhere, amid well-tended gardens.

The beach is soft golden sand, and very peaceful - somewhat less so at weekends when Puerto Plata folk arrive for the day, to play merengue music and drink rum. There is good potential for walking, cycling or horse-riding, with stables within the Club grounds.

Guests who want a change can share taxi transport to Puerto Plata for shopping, or to Playa Dorada for a different style of beach. The round trip to Playa Dorada costs around

£14, which isn't so bad if shared between four or six passengers. Two nights a week – from 8 till 11.30 p.m. - there is free transport to the Jack Tar Casino at Playa Dorada. If you'd rather dance than gamble, there's an excellent disco in the same building.

3.7 Take a trip

East along the coast

The long golden beach of **Cabarete** lies about eight miles east of Sosúa. Thanks to its excellent wind conditions, Cabarete's bay – protected by a reef – is paradise for boardsailing, and is rated among the world's top ten windsurfing sites. Winds freshen up best in the afternoon. Here the windsurfers can find serious championship competition. The Professional Boardsailing Association (PBA) holds the Caribbean leg of an annual World Tour in Cabarete every June, drawing top international sportsmen.

With several kilometres of coconut lined beaches, Cabarete caters mainly for younger watersport devotees, and is specially popular with French Canadians. Charming beachfront inns and small restaurants line the through road, just a step from the dozen windsurf schools and rental operations. Cabarete cannot spread in depth, as the highway is just part of a narrow strip between the Atlantic and a fresh water lagoon. Rowing boats can be hired at the lagoon, to provide a relaxed floating platform for bird watching.

Serving the region is the 9-hole Costa Azul golf course. Another nine holes are planned. In the area, several new and large resorts are under development.

Gaspar Hernández is a typical Dominican market centre with 7,000 population. Countrymen come early morning with their chickens, eggs, beef, pork, fruit, vegetables and milk. They arrive to the pavement market on donkeys, horses, mules and on light trucks. By mid morning, nothing remains except litter. Among the village facilities are a primary school and a public hospital.

The surrounding region is dairy country. Pure Holsteins or Friesians get sick easily, so they are cross bred with hump backed Brahmans from India, which are better suited to the climate. Grazing in lush meadows, the cattle share the scenery with numerous white egrets.

Many field boundaries are marked by acacia trees, which are easily planted. Workers merely cut off a branch, stick it in the ground, and within short time it has struck roots. On hill slopes are piñon trees which originated from Cuba, and yield tasty pine nuts.

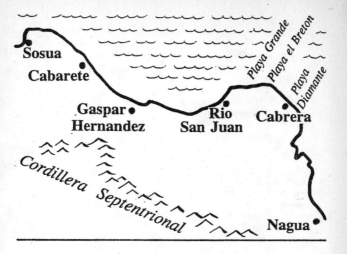

The Amber Coast
Sosua to Samana

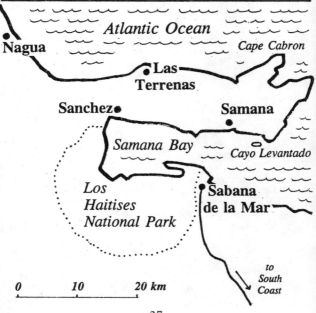

There are many roadside shacks, one room dwellings thatched with palm leaves, mostly on a concrete foundation but very shabby. Some have a horse, donkey or mule tethered in the parking area, with cheerful families of country chickens that wander beneath banana trees. Fruit stands offer cold coconut juice.

A popular sightseeing halt is **The Plantation**, which features a guided circuit of fruit and nut trees and crops. The big commercial plantations are located in other regions, but this enterprise shows how coffee and cocoa beans are grown, and the cultivation of bananas, pineapples, papayas and mangoes.

Continuing east, the road passes many superb beaches such as Magante, and then reaches the small market town of **Río San Juan**. Its highlight is the **Gri Gri Lagoon**. Motor launches take visitors through a dense belt of mangroves. Perched on their curious roots in salt or brackish water, mangroves stabilize coastlines by retaining sediments. They are important breeding areas for fish and invertebrates, and provide a habitat for migrant and resident birds. Frogs and wildfowl live among the mangrove roots, while hundreds of egrets nest high above.

When it's feeding time in the egret colony, there is great squawking from the young as parent birds shuttle back and forth. Vultures glide overhead, or watch from the bare branches of dead trees. With a telephoto lens, you can easily get dramatic wildlife pictures. If the tide is right, it's possible to visit the Cueva de las Golondrinas, home base for a myriad swallows.

Playa Grande, near Río San Juan and 50 miles from Puerto Plata airport, is a long and gorgeous beach backed by coconut and palm trees. It's a classic tropical paradise with golden sand, turquoise water, and waves. At the moment there is nil development. It's just a place for serious sunbathing, with no toilet or changing room facilities. However, beach tent vendors can grill hamburgers or freshly caught fish, and sell you beer, Coke or piña colada.

Big plans are afoot, to convert the zone into another Playa Dorada. Acquired by the Central Bank in 1974, the area awaits investment. As a first stage, an 18-hole Robert Trent Jones-designed golf course will be the central focus, with major hotel resorts already past the project stage.

The coastal road continues, with access to a string of magnificent isolated beaches, such as La Preciosa, El Bretón (on Old French Cape), followed by Playa Diamante. **Cabrera** is almost a village, where simple inns and restaurants are beginning to mushroom. The Nagua Coast features more than 8 miles of continuous sands.

Besides its beaches, the region offers other attractions such as the Virgin of the Cave (a natural rock formation, in a roadside cave), ancient cliffs, and lovely country scenes.

Cattle ranching is the main activity, with important production of cheese and other dairy products.

The Samaná Peninsula

At the extreme east of the Atlantic coast, the Samaná peninsula offers the country's most superb white-sand beaches, set against a mountainous backdrop of three million coconut trees. Twenty miles of unexploited sands stretch along the northern shores, from Las Terrenas to Cape Cabrón. But there is no coastal road. Instead, the highway from Nagua cuts across the neck of the peninsula, to hug Samaná Bay from Sánchez to the town of Samaná itself.

From the port of Samaná you can embark on whale-watching cruises, or take a trip to the Robinson Crusoe island of Cayo Levantado, or cross the Bay by passenger ferry to Sabana de la Mar, which is starting point for a visit to Los Haitises National Park. But access to Los Haitises is more feasible from the south.

Although lightly populated, the strategic harbour of Samaná has several times played an important role in history. In the Bay of Arrows (Bahía de las Flechas) Christopher Columbus and his men were greeted by a hail of arrows from the local Ciguayo Indians. This event in 1493 is credited as the first battle in world history between Indians and Europeans. Columbus had fewer problems in the previous year during his first voyage, when he pulled in here to take on drinking water for the journey back to Spain. Following the Columbus trail, many trans-Atlantic yachts tie up here today for supplies.

The town itself dates from 1756, when settlers arrived from the Canary Islands. The government aim was to forestall conquest by French buccaneers. Then in the 1820's several thousand freed American slaves settled here, financed by abolitionist groups in Philadelphia. Their descendants today are bilingual, speaking Spanish and a 19th-century English of the Deep South. They have surnames like Smith, Brown, Jones and King.

With the arrival of tourism, a flourishing local activity is diving for black coral, and converting it into souvenirs. Help save the environment, and *don't* buy. Import of this endangered species is illegal into Europe and USA. Coral reefs need protection.

For the perfect beach, most visitors take a 20-minute boat ride to Cayo Levantado – a dreamy paradise of white sandy beaches and crystal-clear water with every shade of blue. A popular nickname is Bacardi Island, ever since it was used as location for a rum commercial. Bring snorkel gear, or hire some, to view the colourful underwater life. The local specialty of fish in a coconut sauce is often served at beach barbecues.

The waters around Samaná peninsula are the annual travel destination of over 2,000 humpback whales who cruise down from Maine, Greenland and Iceland between mid-December and mid-March. Their journey is motivated by a desire for mating. It's a huge whale-marriage market, where males and females gather and courtship begins – often with several males eager for one desirable female. After mating, there's a quickie divorce and the whales return to solitary life. After 12 months' gestation, the females come back to Samaná to give birth. The year afterwards, with young off their flippers, they return once more for another courtship session.

West along the coast
About 17 miles from Puerto Plata is **Luperón**, a 20,000-population town named after a 19th-century general who led a rebellion in 1866 to restore the Republic. Apart from the all-inclusive Luperón Beach Resort, there's not much reason to linger. However, it's an angler's paradise, with good facilities for deep sea fishing. Luperón Bay offers a large and safe yacht marina. Some boat tours are based here.

For instance, regular trips are available aboard a 55-ft double decked party boat. The Tropical Dream Cruise idea is to sail for 90 minutes to Cambiaso Beach, which is otherwise inaccessible by road. Here you step back a few centuries. Close by is a typical small village of 80 people who live in tiny huts without electricity, but surrounded by beautiful and untamed beaches.

The arrival of the boat is greeted by live musicians. Donkeys are lined up for rides across the village and the two main beaches. There is ample time for snorkelling, while a barbecue lunch is prepared.

Isabela
Along rough roads west of Luperón is La Isabela, founded by Christopher Columbus in 1493 and named after the Spanish queen. This was the first European settlement to be established in the New World. The previous year's settlement of 39 sailors in present-day Haiti had disappeared.

But within six years the 1500 colonists at La Isabela had fallen away through disease and general bickering. They either went home to Spain, or relocated to Santo Domingo in the south, or set up as cattle ranchers elsewhere. Archaeologists have done their best, but there's little to see on the site except a general outline to show where the main buildings were located.

Estero Hondo
Another remote location: a wilderness beach where a group of anti-Trujillo guerrillas disembarked in 1959 in a failed attempt to dislodge the dictator. An estuary, designated as a nature park, is a habitat for the West Indian manatee – an endangered species which now has better chance of survival, thanks to tourism.

The manatee is a kind of sea cow which dines off seaweed. These gentle grey-brown giants, measuring up to 13 feet long and weighing well over a ton, inhabit shallow coastal waters, lagoons and estuaries in Florida and the Caribbean. Formerly in this area the manatees were hunted. But a Puerto Plata company called Ecoturisa has persuaded the local villagers to protect rather than kill.

The estuary, thick with mangrove vegetation, is explored by motor launch. There are tropical birds to spot. From a floating observation platform, there will hopefully be sight of manatees, though nothing can be guaranteed. Meanwhile, the locals are involved – preparing a barbecue, or manning the boats.

There is full cooperation from the villagers who now realise that ecological tourism can give them a sustainable income – so long as there are manatees. The whole project has gained the coveted Thomson award for Best Eco Tour, aimed at rewarding environment-friendly tourism.

Monte Cristi

Close to the Haitian border, this area is flat and arid, more suited to goat-herding than cattle ranching. The promontory of El Morro is claimed to have inspired Alexander Dumas to write *The Count of Monte-Cristo*. Formerly, Monte Cristi was the leading Spanish port on the north coast. The remains of 179 sunken galleons litter the seabed in the area. Further round, on Manzanillo Bay, is an international free trade and industrial Zone.

Across the island

From the Amber Coast there are several sightseeing options inland, mainly to include **Santiago**. The available routes pass over the northern range of mountains – the Cordillera Septentrional – which mark the boundary between the provinces of Puerto Plata and Santiago. Beyond that mountain range, the Yaque River flows through the Cibao Valley, one of the Dominican Republic's most fertile areas.

Sightseeing of Santiago may be the prime purpose of the journey, but the beautiful cross-country drive is itself worth the trip. It's a good chance to see a cross-section of the rural lifestyle, with memorable sights every mile of the route.
On a one-day excursion, it's also possible to visit **Santo Domingo** from the north coast. With an early start and breakfast en route, the four-hour journey across the island still leaves time to skim the historic highlights of the capital. Obviously it makes a very long day, but the trip is very rewarding.

Whichever your chosen route inland, there is great interest in the wayside villages and scattered cabins. Housing conditions are very poor, but the setting and the views are fabulous. Each tiny cabin has its patch of maize, vegetable plot, backyard banana trees, a few pigs and free-range country chickens. A mule or donkey may be sheltered beneath a mango tree, while a tethered family goat grazes on the highway verge.

From roadside stands, families earn a sideline income by selling any surplus to passing motorists: bananas, cashew nuts, fresh vegetables. Some palm-thatched huts offer refreshments, and small shops operate from lock-ups the size of garden sheds. Many premises are decorated in the corporate colours of 7-Up or Coca-Cola, Pepsi or Sprite. There are even wayside discos, and fast-food stands that sell grilled pork and crackling, cooked by open fires.

Agile cattle forage up one-in-three slopes, against a background of mountains and brilliant flamboyant trees. On the forested hillsides are white pine trees with very long trunks that could make instant telegraph poles. Other hillsides are terraced and planted with pineapple. Bridges cross ravines, where it's impossible to see the river below, because of the dense overhang of green vegetation. Some of the side valleys look like untamed jungle.

After the hill scenery, the road emerges onto the central plain of the Cibao Valley, totally ringed with mountains. Small farms look beautiful with their diversity of trees. Cattle ranching of the north coastal plain has given way to cash-crop country, with fields of banana, coffee, rice, tobacco and sweet potato. Farm labourers wear baseball caps – a reminder of the Dominican Republic's national sport, with Santiago standing high in the league.

Santiago de los Caballeros

On the outskirts of Santiago is a bustling farmers' market, serving the local trade. Fruit stands are beautifully laid out with citrus, long bunches of ripe bananas, pyramids of pineapple, and colourful tropical vegetables that are rarely seen in Europe.

Santiago is an industrial city, deeply involved in the manufacture or processing of the Cibao Valley's field crops. In light-industrial suburbs are orange-juice factories, cigarette plants and varied food-packing operations such as manufacture of chocolate and spaghetti. More than 10,000 people work in the Industrial Free Zone.

Santiago sightseeing normally includes a visit to several commercial operations – cigar manufacture, a rum distillery and a pottery.

A typical visit to La Aurora cigar factory shows the manufacture of hand-rolled cigars, mainly for export to USA. In the highest-grade cigars they use half Cuban tobacco and half Dominican. A typical worker can roll 250 cigars a day, and earns about US $72 a week. At La Aurora factory they also make Marlborough and other international cigarette brands under license. Presidente beer and Heiniken beer are brewed in the same factory complex.

Elsewhere is the intoxicating air of a rum warehouse, where 20,000 barrels are stored under one roof. Out of Dominica's huge production of rum, 95% is drunk as a local thirst-quencher, leaving only 5% for the rest of the world.

Santiago, population 500,000, is the republic's second largest city, and the second oldest, founded in 1498 though its location has shifted twice.

The city's central plaza is Duarte Park, ringed by narrow traffic-jammed streets. Horse carriage rides make a gentle circuit of the area, with its colonial style buildings and fanciful colouring of Victorian houses. The principal shopping street is Calle El Sol, which starts from Duarte Park. Along that street is the Mercado, filled with handicraft vendors who expect you to haggle.

On the museum front, the most interesting is the Tomés Morel Folklore Museum, with a wide selection of carnival masks. If you want to nose deeper into the history of smoke, a Tobacco Museum is located on Calle 30 de Marzo, near Calle del Sol.

Apart from Santiago's role as an industrial centre, the city is home to a top-ranking University run by the Catholic church. The most prominent landmark is the Heroes Monument, which commemorates the patriots who helped restore the republic in 1864. It was built in 1946, during the reign of dictator Trujillo. The splendid hilltop location overlooks the entire region, offering a great panorama over the city.

3.8 Nightlife

In the Puerto Plata area you'll never be short of evening entertainment – quite apart from what's on the programme of your own hotel. There are plentiful nightclubs, such as Casa del Sol and Medusa in Sosúa; and Bogarts, Andromeda, Charlie's and Crazy Moon in Playa Dorada. A cover charge is payable for entrance to all night clubs – around £3 in Sosúa and £5 in Puerto Plata.

For dining out, check the restaurant listings in the local tourist weekly publication "Puerto Plata News".

Casinos

There are five easily accessible casinos – three in Playa Dorada, and one each in Puerta Plata and Sosúa. You don't have to be a big spender. There are no entrance fees. You can just saunter around, looking, and maybe throw caution to the winds on a US 25-cent slot machine. Drinks and cigarettes are free for players, but not for onlookers. If you gamble in pesos, any winnings are paid in pesos; gamble in dollars, and the payout is dollars.

Each casino is linked to a big hotel – normally located on the fringe of each complex, so that visitors can arrive without going through the individual hotel security system.

The largest casino is at Jack Tar Village, and is built like a Greek temple. It offers the full range of blackjack, poker, roulette, baccarat and craps, plus the usual array of slots. Inside the same building is the Caligula Disco and a gourmet restaurant called "Elaines".

Another large casino is located at the Playa Dorada Hotel – very spacious and air conditioned. Like most of the others, it opens at 4 p.m. and closes at 4 a.m. The smaller casino attached to Paradise Hotel has all the standard games, but no slots.

At the Puerto Plata Beach Resort, located on the Malecón, the small but well equipped casino is usually quite busy, possibly due to its easy-to-find location. Sosúa's casino is attached to Playa Chiquita Hotel.

Discos
At the Caligula Disco, entrance is free for Jack Tar residents, but drinks are not. Non-residents pay about US $4 for entrance, while drinks start at US $2.

Discos attached to other hotels of Playa Dorada mostly follow a similar policy and price-scale. Dress is smart casual – admission may be refused for anyone arriving in shorts and T-shirt. Doors open at 9 p.m., and close at 4 a.m.

The Ambrosia at Puerto Plata Village charges higher admission, but then serves unlimited drinks all night, with seating capacity for 200.

The Andromeda at Heavens Hotel is much larger, seating 500. Capacity of Top's Disco at Playa Naco is even higher, somewhere around 700 people. Crazy Moon is attached to Paradise Hotel and seats 350, and the Obsession Disco Club is close by, near the Playa Dorada Plaza. The smallest disco is Charlie's at Playa Dorada Hotel, with space for only 150 persons. In downtown Puerto Plata, consider a visit to Orion.

Chapter Four

Discover Santo Domingo

4.1 Introduction to Santo Domingo

Explore the Caribbean's most historic city. The colonial sector of Santo Domingo is the first European-type city built in the New World. The oldest city in the Americas was founded in 1496 by Bartholemew, the brother of Christopher Columbus. Owing to its central location in the Caribbean, Santo Domingo became the base for expeditions throughout the western hemisphere. For the first half of the 16th century it was the major port-of-call en route between Spain and South America, but was then largely replaced by Havana.

The capital of the Dominican Republic can boast of the first cathedral, fortress, hospital, monastery, university, palace and street in the Americas. Most of that rich heritage is still standing, even though the English pirate Sir Francis Drake set everything ablaze in 1586.

For 1992, to celebrate the 500th anniversary of The Discovery, the Dominican government made a special effort to restore the historic monuments. That job was well done, and today's visitor can recapture much of the early 16th-century character.

All the great Spanish voyagers spent time here, including Hernán Cortés, the conqueror of Mexico; Ponce de León who colonized Puerto Rico and explored Florida; Balboa, the first European to sight the eastern shore of the Pacific Ocean; Pizarro who opened up Columbia and Peru; and Velazquez who conquered and governed Cuba. So much history was launched from this site!

There's even a possibility that Columbus himself is buried here. He died 1506 in Valladolid, Spain, but his remains went on travelling. First he was buried in Seville. Then, to fulfill his last wishes, his burial urn was supposedly moved to Santo Domingo Cathedral in 1544. When Spain lost the colony in 1795, some relics were exhumed and possibly removed to Havana, and then maybe returned for interment in Seville Cathedral. However, there were probably mix-ups in the itinerary, bones are easily confused, and Santo Domingo is among the dozen or more sites which still claim possession.

On October 6, 1992, the huge and costly Columbus Lighthouse was inaugurated – a towering modern structure on the ground-plan of a cross. The reputed bones of Columbus were again moved from Santo Domingo Cathedral, into this new monument which also houses a dozen international displays devoted to 500 years of exploration.

To discover the Santo Domingo of four or five centuries ago, a stroll down the cobblestoned streets of the old sector is full of sightseeing delights. The Colonial Zone has been proclaimed by the United Nations as the city of "cultural heritage of the New World."

However, Santo Domingo does not live in the past. As a bustling modern port, and city of two million, the capital sprawls across both sides of the River Ozama. Today's city ranges from shanty dwellings to completely 20th-century architecture set amid spacious parks. There is good shopping potential, and the liveliest nightlife in the Caribbean. But, for the visitor, it's the Colonial Zone which is most worth exploring.

4.2 Arrival & orientation

Air travellers arrive at Las Américas International Airport, 19 miles east of the city centre. A prestigious highway called Avenida Las Américas runs parallel to the coast, lined with palm trees. It crosses the Ozama River over Duarte Bridge, to reach the heart of the modern city.

This also is the arrival route for visitors who come in from resorts along the southern coast – Boca Chica, 20 miles east; Juan Dolio 40 miles; La Romana 70 miles.

From Puerto Plata on the north coast, the distance is 135 miles – a 4-hour road journey, with arrival into the north-western suburbs.

The east side of River Ozama was the original site of Santo Domingo, until it was moved to the river's west bank in 1502. There the Governor Nicolas de Ovando began building of the fortified colonial city, with its stone houses and government offices, which still survive intact almost 500 years later.

The port of Santo Domingo lies at the river mouth, where cruise-ship passengers disembark. That's the location chosen by the original settlers. The first three bridges are named after the founding fathers of the Dominican Republic – Mella, Duarte and Sánchez. On the east side of the river are three major sightseeing highlights: the Columbus Lighthouse and Los Tres Ojos (The Three Eyes) at each end of the long Mirador East Park; and the National Aquarium, fairly close by the seashore.

Everything else worth seeing is on the west bank - particularly the compact area of the 16th-century Colonial Zone, designed on city-grid pattern, and very easily explored on foot.

Around twenty major 4- and 5-star hotels are located close to George Washington Avenue, which forms part of the Malecón – the five-mile seaside highway and promenade running west from the Colonial Zone.

Closest to the Colonial Zone is the Sheraton Hotel, which also features a prestigious casino. Under joint ownership are the Hispaniola Hotel and the Hotel Santo Domingo, which combine into a virtually self-contained resort with luxurious rooms, pools and a Vegas-style casino. These hotels reflect the city's double importance as a business and political centre, and also a tourist and nightlife destination in its own right.

Despite its long seafront, Santo Domingo has no beaches except for a surfers' rendezvous called Guibia. The lack of beach space explains why great numbers of local residents stream out to Boca Chica at weekends.

4.3 Colonial Zone

Columbus Park is the best starting-point for exploring the Colonial Sector. A statue of the admiral in heroic pose faces Santo Domingo Cathedral. On a corner of the park rises the white steeple of the former City Hall, now restored for other purposes. It marks the beginning of El Conde Street, an upmarket shopping precinct which carves cleanly across the walled city to the historic El Conde Gate.

From Columbus Park, all the highlights of the Colonial Zone are within a few minutes' walk.

4.3.1 Santo Domingo Cathedral
was founded in early 16th century, the first in the western hemisphere. It has an unfinished look, partly due to its rough-cut coral stone, scarred by time and occasional cannon-balls. The architectural style is mixed – Renaissance facade with an interior blend of Romanesque and Gothic. The cornerstone was laid by Diego, the son of Columbus. Both men have been buried here, though the present location of their bones is disputed.

Drake and his men camped in the cathedral when they plundered the city in 1586. One of the 14 chapels was used as Drake's bedroom while he supervized the removal of gold and silver altarpieces, the treasury and varied works of art.

Curators are strict that knees and shoulders should be covered. Entrance is barred to anyone in shorts or wearing sleeveless shirts. Creative use of scarves can overcome the problem.

The charming pedestrian street of **Callejón de los Nichos**, between the Cathedral and the Fortress, is lined with decorative tropical trees. Many of the men who made New World history have lived along this street, and also along the Calle las Damas at the end.

4.3.2 Ozama Fortress and Tower of Homage

The fortress is the most ancient military building of the Americas. Work began in 1503, under the governorship of Nicolás de Ovando. The main gate was constructed in 1787, during the reign of Carlos 111. The Tower of Homage served as a prison, even until recent times when dictator Trujillo gaoled his opponents. In the grounds is a dramatic bronze statue of Gonzalo Fernández de Oviedo, the fortress governor from 1533-57, but better known as a great historian of the Indies.

Adjoining the Fortress is **Casa de Bastidas**, a group of shops, museums and galleries.

4.3.3 Calle Las Damas

Out of the fortress, a stroll to the right along Calle Las Damas is delightful, and shouldn't be missed if time permits. Every house and building is crammed with history, along this oldest street in the New World, running from the Fortress to the Alcazar. In the 16th century, most members of the viceroy's court resided here. Their ladies would stroll out for evening promenades, in a romantic stage setting of cobble-stoned street, wrought-iron lanterns and Moorish archways. Most of the buildings are labelled with historical plaques.

On the corner with Callejón de los Nichos, look closely at the black and white limestone building, restored in 1978. It is traditionally known as the **House of Hermán Cortés**. It was original built in 1502 to house important state institutions of the time. Today it's used as the Maison de France, in the cultural service of the French Embassy. Stroll inside to view the lovely courtyards, with trees and foliage.

Close by, a typical town mansion now functions as HQ of a booklovers' society. A neighbouring building is the Don Carlos House, operating as a low-profile gift shop.

Opposite is the **Hostal Nicolás de Ovando**. This elegant 45-room hotel was Governor Ovando's residence when he was directing the building of Santo Domingo. The hostal has been restored to its full 16th century glory with courtyards, Andalusian fountains and balconies.

It's worth dropping in for a drink at the poolside bar. The Hostal is built right on the city walls, offering good views over the river. The premises have been extended by taking in the white building next door, which belonged to the wealthy Dávila family. Restored by the government in 1974, it incorporates a very charming tavern.

Across the street is the **National Pantheon**, originally built in 1755 as a Jesuit monastery church. It was restored in 1955 during the Trujillo dictatorship, and transformed into a mausoleum for the famous. Next door was another Jesuit building, now converted to other use.

Around the corner, along Mercedes Street, are several more gracious 16th-century mansions. Next to the House

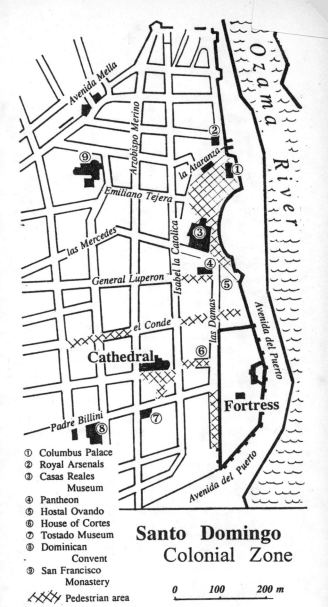

of the Jesuits is the **House of the Gargoyles**, which adjoins the **House of Don Juan de Villoria**.

Opposite is the side entrance to the **Museo de las Casas Reales** – open daily except Monday, entrance about US $1. This superb museum covers all aspects of the island's social, economic and military history between 1492 and 1821. Here you can view the fantastic treasure hoard from a Spanish galleon – the *Conde de Tolosa* – which sank in deep water off Samaná on the north-east coast. There are good collections of 16th century art, furniture and military uniforms, and displays relating to pirates and tobacco. The building itself originated as the Palace of the Captains – a Court of Appeal and seat of Spanish colonial government for 300 years.

On the broad esplanade outside is a **Sundial** dating from 1753. Cannon are displayed along the fortress parapet which overlooks the Ozama River, where early Spanish ships moored almost 500 years ago. Some imitation city walls were built by Trujillo to replace parts of the original. Further along, on the high riverbank, is the Alcazar of Colon.

4.3.4 Columbus Alcazar

Diego Columbus, son of Christopher, had married well, to the aristocratic Maria de Toledo. When he arrived in 1509 as first viceroy in the New World, he gave priority to building a 22-room palace of native coral, to house his court and wife in suitable style. For over 60 years, this Columbus family home was centre of the Spanish court. Here were planned all the great 16th-century expeditions.

Until the early 18th century the Alcazar remained in the Columbus family. But then it fell into disrepair, was used as a warehouse, and was abandoned. Earthquakes finished it off.

Total reconstruction came from 1957 onwards, and today's building is a faithful reproduction thanks to all available pictorial and written records. Likewise, the furnishings are authentic 16th century, and the rooms are set out precisely as described in records: from the kitchen, to the music room, viceregal bedrooms, and the splendid reception room with a model of the Santa Maria.

Steps lead down from the Alcazar to **Ataranza Street**. The original buildings from 1507 were designed for storage of naval supplies. The current conversion into shops, art galleries, taverns and restaurants is utterly charming, with wrought-iron grill work on balconies and windows.

4.3.5 Casa de Tostado

Just behind Santo Domingo Cathedral is Clergymen's Place – a peaceful location, leading into the colourful little passage of Clergymen's Lane. Turn right along Calle Padre Billini, to reach the Casa de Tostado. This former

Archbishop's Palace now houses a collection of 19th-century family possessions and furniture.

Open daily except Wed, 9-14.30 hrs, the serene 16th-century residence gives a good impression of a wealthy Victorian lifestyle. An upstairs reception room displays antique hand operated sewing machines. The magnificent high-ceilinged sitting room has ultra-wide Gothic windows for a constant cooling breeze. A wide paved gallery looks onto a shady courtyard.

Further along Calle Padre Billini, facing the **Convent of the Dominicans** is a statue of **Juan Pablo Duarte**, founder of the Dominican Republic.

Monastery of Saint Francis
Established in 1514 as the New World's first monastery, it was looted and set ablaze by Drake in 1586. Today the hilltop ruins – located three blocks from La Ataranza – are used as a perfect setting for cultural events.

4.4 Other sights & museums
After the highlights of the Colonial Zone, the most interesting visits are across the river, near the east bank where the original settlement was located.

4.4.1 The Columbus Lighthouse
is the official current resting place of the explorer's remains. White-uniformed naval guards with fixed bayonets are posted permanently around his marble mausoleum. The lighthouse itself was designed in 1931 by an award-winning British architect. Construction was deferred for many years through funding problems, which finally were overcome in readiness for inauguration in October 1992 to mark the 5th centennial of the Columbus voyage.

For a lighthouse, the building is somewhat unusual, more like a pyramid-shaped Aztec shrine in reinforced concrete. The ground-plan is a cross measuring 688 feet long. On the outer walls are the names of men and women who have contributed to the history of the New World. The lighting system projects enormously powerful beams through slits in the roof, to form a gigantic cross in the sky which can be seen 40 miles away.

The length of the building is devoted to galleries that display varied aspects of Discovery. Over twenty countries are represented, including Britain, USA, Japan, Israel, Italy and Spain. One section is dedicated to the history of Columbus and the Lighthouse itself.

Los Tres Ojos de Agua (The Three Eyes of Water) is a natural cave housing three lagoons of transparent turquoise waters on three different levels. A fourth lake has been discovered. Stalactites and stalagmites are viewed through lush tropical vegetation. Take care down the slippery steps! The site is located at the far end of the park which stretches east from the Columbus Lighthouse.

The National Aquarium, located in parkland by the seashore, features a superb collection of tropical fish, beautifully displayed in tanks that show different habitats. A snag: the descriptive notes are entirely in Spanish. But it's still worth spending at least an hour, feasting the eyes. The highlight is to pass through a glassed-in tunnel, enjoying an eyeball panorama of the psychedelic underwater life on a coral reef. Some of the fish are brilliantly coloured, while others are masters of camouflage.

Open daily except Monday, 9.30-18 hrs. Entrance is about one US dollar for foreigners, half price for locals.

4.4.2 *Plaza de la Cultura* is set is a beautifully landscaped park on Maximo Gomez Avenue in the modern sector of the city, close to the big hotels. Highlight of the complex is the **Museum of Dominican Man**, covering pre-Columbian times to the present. Displays illustrate the full range of Dominican life-style, past and present, including voodoo, the diet, carnival and life in a sugarcane village.

Twentieth-century Dominican painters, woodcarvers, sculptors and photographers are represented in the **Museum of Modern Art**. The Plaza also includes the **National Theatre**, the **National Library**, and the **Natural History Museum**.

4.5 Shopping

Obviously a city of two million inhabitants offers a full selection of shopping areas in all price categories.

For a Dominican style of Oxford Street – everything in the department stores at very popular fixed prices – it's an unforgettable experience to visit Mella Avenue, where the average Dominican family goes shopping amid scenes of utter chaos. Street vendors block the narrow pavement with fold-up tables, selling everything from junk jewelry to wrist watches and cassettes.

Amid all this bedlam is **Mercado Modelo**, where broad yellow steps lead to an Art Deco bazaar. It's a public market, built like an aircraft hangar, and is the country's largest centre for stacked craft items and every imaginable souvenir. Haggling is essential. If you can't get a major price cut from the opening quote, another dozen traders are eager for your business along the crowded aisles.

Shopping is much more decorous along **El Conde Street** in the heart of the Colonial Zone, pedestrianized with shops, bars and informal cafés. This oldest shopping street of Santo Domingo runs from the former Town Hall on the corner of Columbus Park, clear across the old city to the **El Conde Gate**.

On 27 February 1844 El Conde Gate had its dramatic share in history, when patriots forced a surrender of the Haitian garrison, and proclaimed an independent Dominican Republic.

In addition to these thoroughfares, there are also many excellent shopping malls in modern areas of the city, such as Plaza Criolla, Plaza Naco, and Galarias Commerciales.

Finally, there are **Duty Free Shops** in Santo Domingo, where you can shop in tranquility for items such as cameras, watches and perfumes. Purchases are made in US dollars and are delivered at the airline terminal upon departure.

Of the two Duty Free Complexes – Tiendas Zona Franca - the handiest is located in the Atarazanas Reales sector of the Colonial Zone, at the bottom end of Vicente Celestino Duarte Street. The other is a seven-store complex at the Centro de los Heroes government centre, on Paul P. Harris and Hippolito Herrera Billini Streets.

4.6 Nightlife

After hours, Santo Domingo comes alive in its nightclubs, bars, discos and casinos – especially along the famed Malecón, the seaside boulevard that never sleeps.

Among local residents, the nightlife schedule is Spanish style: dine from 10 p.m., and head to a disco or casino around midnight. Earlier hours are followed by tourists who haven't adjusted to the afternoon siesta routine.

A number of hotels and bars feature early evening Happy Hours, two drinks for the price of one. Their times differ, so that you could plan a Happy-Hour crawl from 5 p.m. till 8.30. Check the free English-language weekly *Santo Domingo News* for timings and a general calendar of What's Up.

A popular rendezvous is La Guácara Taína, a multi-level cultural centre and disco set in a massive underground cave, with capacity for 1500 people. It's open daily from 9 p.m., with an hour-long folk dance show usually on Tuesday, Thursday and Friday at 10.30 p.m., followed by a Disco Laser till dawn. Merengue bands are featured on Mondays. Entrance of US $10 includes a first drink.

For reservations, and to confirm when the folk shows are operating, phone 530-2662 between 8-17 hrs; or 533-1051 from 17-21 hrs.

Night tour

From Juan Dolio or Boca Chica there are night tours to the capital. You'll see the night sky lit up by the impressive Columbus lighthouse. Then – depending on the tour package - a meal at a good restaurant, with a visit to the Guácara Taína for the folklore show and disco.

The evening would probably include a session at the Hispaniola Casino, where all the usual gaming tables are in full swing: roulette, craps, blackjack and poker. For those who prefer slot machines, there's wide choice of one-arm bandits and electronic card games.

If you want to try elsewhere, there are equally lavish casinos at the Sheraton Hotel or the Embajador, the Ramada Jaragua Resort and several other major hotels.

Chapter Five

The South coast

5.1 Introduction to the Caribbean coast

The Caribbean coast, east of Santo Domingo, offers a series of holiday centres from Boca Chica to Juan Dolio, La Romana and thence to Punta Caña on the eastern shore. Each area offers a totally different holiday experience.

Depending on the day of the week, Boca Chica changes its face. Weekdays it's a relatively quiet resort, which has grown around the original tiny fishing village. At weekends it bubbles with all the vivacity of the Dominicana life-style.

The reason? Only 20 miles east of Santo Domingo, Boca Chica is the first-choice beach for the capital's two million residents. For a Sunday outing, thousands of families pour in, to convert Boca Chica into one of the liveliest waterfronts on the island. It's a great place for meeting the locals.

The converse applies. Boca Chica is a good base for making trips into the capital, to explore Santo Domingo in greater depth. Public transport is frequent.

Juan Dolio is a complete contrast. Almost 40 miles from the capital, it's a ribbon development of beach hotel-resorts along a string of beautiful sandy coves. The outgoing waves of weekend trippers from the capital are only a few ripples by the time they reach Juan Dolio, where the beaches are occupied almost totally by Europeans and North Americans. The coastal highway is just a few minutes' stroll inland, and provides good access to the sightseeing highlights of the region.

For total escape, seriously wealthy holidaymakers head past the sugar-cane plantations and rolling countryside of La Romana to Casa de Campo, the ultimate playground for sport lovers. Privacy and luxury reign throughout the resort's 7,000 tropical acres.

Twenty years ago, Punta Caña and Bávaro on the country's isolated eastern tip was no more than a lonesome stretch of prime beachfront bush. Today that diamond in the rough has been shaped into a brilliant tourist enclave.

Along the so-called Coconut Coast are some 20 miles of fine white sands, crystal-clear shallow waters, and a coral reef that stretches for over four miles. Road access is poor, but many groups fly in from Santo Domingo or by direct charter to an international-grade airport only five minutes' drive from Punta Caña.

The entire area is sparsely populated. Guests are mainly those who just want to relax and enjoy watersports and the on-site entertainment, in self-contained isolation from the rest of the country. With ecology in mind, development is low density, with no building higher than three stories. The zone's 300,000 coconut trees are safe.

5.2 Orientation

In the eastern provinces of the Dominican Republic there are only five towns of any size – San Pedro de Macorís; La Romana; Higüey; El Seibo; and Hato Mayor. They are mainly market centres for a region which depends on the harvesting and processing of sugar cane, rice and cotton. Sugar is the most important, with huge plantations. Six major sugar mills refine the crop, including three mills in Macorís, and one each in La Romana and Boca Chica.

The America Highway hugs the coast – a beautiful drive throughout. It starts out from Santo Domingo as a spacious dual carriageway, but then gradually tapers off into a second-grade road where drivers swerve around the pot-holes.

This highway feeds lesser routes into the interior, which becomes very rugged indeed if you're aiming for the Bay of Samaná to the north, for access to the Haitises National Park.

Smoother travel is offered by the numerous rivers which drain from hills of the Cordillera Oriental in the north of the peninsula. Pleasant tourist excursions are based on up-river boat-trips, often combined with jeep or horseback safaris to a ranch buried deep in the countryside.

In the furthest south-east corner is the Parque Nacional del Este. The only concession to tourism is a 42-mile track around the National Park coastline, with no facilities except a few huts for overnight shelter. A tough hiker, carrying his own supplies, could complete the walk in three days. The Park also includes the island of Saona, which can be visited on day-trip boat excursions.

5.3 The Caribbean coast resorts

Boca Chica's appeal is a very long beach of powdery white sand and a calm lagoon, described as the island's largest swimming pool. Enclosed by a reef, the waters couldn't be safer for children. Paddlers can wade out a hundred yards without getting their shoulders wet. Waves are banished to the other side of the reef.

In most parts of the beach, the sand reaches way back to a fringe of rustling coconut palms. Thatched beach huts add to the available shade.

Boca Chica's development as an international resort can partly be credited to dictator Trujillo. During his reign, Trujillo liked to come to this modest fishing-village location for an easily-accessible break from Santo Domingo. A 30-room Hamaca Hotel was built in a prime beach-front location, and the third floor was reserved exclusively for the Presidential suite.

Members of his entourage, and wealthy people who found it useful to be around, built villa retreats in the area, which thus became the top people's resort.

With the fall of Trujillo in 1961, Boca Chica was no longer fashionable. Villas were sold off and became guest-houses and restaurants. Hotel Hamaca went downhill, and was wrecked in 1979 by a hurricane. More recently the hotel has been totally rebuilt and extended to 5-star status in something like Moorish style.

Meanwhile democracy and increased mobility introduced the idea of Boca Chica as a weekend escape from Santo Domingo. In more recent times, the gorgeous beach has also been discovered by international tour operators from Canada, Germany, Italy, Switzerland and other European countries. In turn there has been development of international-grade hotels.

This background history explains the wide choice of bars, restaurants and fast-food operations in every grade and price-range, all tightly grouped together. Catering both for local visitors from the capital, and for a range of international clients, the eating places feature every imaginable cuisine - from Dominican and Mexican to Spanish, French, Chinese, you-name-it.

Likewise, beach vendors cater both for local and international customers. Seated at a beachside bar, you are the target for a constant stream of salesmen of postcards, amber necklaces, T-shirts, paintings, fruit, toffee-apples. Vendors worry about the sun on your head, and implore you to protect yourself with a straw hat. Musical trios come serenading, a new group every ten minutes. It's worth having a pocket-full of peso coins, to persuade them to move on.

On Sundays, all Dominican family life is right there on the beach. Some families bring a hammock, which they stretch between palm-trees. Inflated inner tubes are available for hire, all ready for a child's voyage of discovery around the lagoon. The dominant sound is of music, simultaneously from a dozen different sources — radio, cassette players, live musicians. If you hear shouting and a succession of loud cracks, it's not a Dominican shoot-out, but a friendly game of dominoes.

On weekdays the decibel count dwindles, but there's still plenty of action at the international-grade beach hotels, each with a manicured stretch of sand adjoining its foreshore. Horse-riding, for instance, is a popular option. A local stables offers one-hour rides for around US $15. For more experienced riders, horseback safaris can last from five to seven hours, including a break for lunch.

Boca Chica can provide a full range of water-sports, including scuba diving at La Caleta underwater National Park, near Santo Domingo Airport. The attraction is a boat called "Hickory", deliberately sunk in 1984 to create an artificial reef. Near the wreck are anchors and cannons from Spanish galleons. The site has matured into an ideal setting for deep-sea diving.

Other boat exursions are made to the off-shore islands of La Matica and Los Pinos, with the chance of snorkelling, surfing and fishing. A regular Sunset Cruise includes drinks and merengue music.

Depending on the season, deep-sea fishing is organised for blue marlin or kingfish, about 25 miles out. There are six lines on a boat and room for three onlookers. Instruction is given. December until March is best for blue marlin; April until July for kingfish. Blue marlin weigh up to 150 pounds; kingfish from 25 to 100 pounds.

Juan Dolio is a beachfront tourism enclave with a good range of small hotels, self-catering bungalows and larger all-inclusive complexes. The shoreline is divided into a series of little bays, each having its resort hotel, with restaurant development in the second line, back to the main highway. The entire development is screened by palm trees. Beyond the highway are broad vistas of sugar cane.

An air-conditioned Metro bus runs into Santo Domingo at 9.30 every morning, returning at 16 hrs, for a return fare of about US $5. Typical prices for water-sports, mostly per hour, are: sailboat US $8; catamaran $14; wind-surfing $8: kayak $6; snorkelling $5. Some of the resort hotels operate on the all-inclusive package basis, with sport facilities at no extra charge.

The total clarity of the water, all along the coast, has sparked interest in scuba-diving. The Playa Caribe Diving Center is the largest diving school in the area, with excursions operated to Catalina Island and Bayahibe.

The nearest town is **San Pedro De Macorís**, which grew in the 19th century on the sugar and rum industry, and the export of bananas from its harbour on the River Iguamo. More recently San Pedro has successfully diversified through an industrial free zone. The daily fruit and vegetable market offers good photo-making potential.

The town takes great pride in its local baseball team, and can claim dozens of former players who have made it good in USA. The Dominican season is from October to January. San Pedro is also a university town, with a highly reputed medical school which draws students from other Caribbean islands.

La Romana is one of the country's cleanest cities, established as a sugar production centre in the early 20th century, and home of the world's second largest sugar mill. The sugar interests — including 107,000 acres of cane fields — were formerly owned by the US conglomerate, Gulf + Western, who had the vision to diversify.

The most imaginative diversification was to buy up 7,000 acres of scrub land, three miles east of La Romana, and convert it into **Caso de Campo**, billed as the "Caribbean's most complete resort". The complex has 750 rooms, spread either in the central location or in highly luxurious villas that include the services of a maid and butler.

Within the site is the widest possible range of sporting activities: three world-class golf courses designed by Peter Dye; a tennis club which has been described as "the Wimbledon of the Caribbean"; 14 swimming pools; an equestrian centre featuring a Dude Ranch and a Rodeo area; three fields for playing polo during the November to May season, with over 500 trained ponies available; a Shooting Centre developed over 150 acres of wild vegetation — the world's largest private sporting clays facility; and all the usual water sports.

All these sports are also open to non-residents, at appropriate fees. Visitors merely check at the Information Centre for the activities they wish to tackle. Free minibuses circle the complex every 15 minutes, or a 4-seater golf cart can be rented for $30 a day.

Another major attraction attached to Casa de Campo is Altos De Chavón, built 1976 in the style of a 16th century Mediterranean village. The Church of St. Stanislaus in the centre is dedicated to Poland's patron saint, and had the full blessing of Pope John Paul 11. The main building material of rough-cast coral stone is similar to that used in Santo Domingo's Colonial Zone. Already the site has matured well, with brilliant flowering plants and shrubs. The 16th-century illusion is complete, even to the 16th-century Spanish disco at the entrance.

The village is totally committed to the arts, with a thriving art community affiliated to New York's Parsons School of Design. A regional Museum of Archaeology documents the island's pre-Columbian cultural heritage. The Art Gallery is a showcase for emerging and established painters, sculptors and photographers, Dominican and international. The Performing Arts Complex is centred on a 5,000-seat Greek-style amphitheatre, where stars such as Frank Sinatra have performed.

In the nearby fishing village of Bayahibe is the Italian-run resort of **Club Dominicus**, sited on one of the country's best beaches.

Higüey is the nearest town to the beautiful but remote beaches of Macao, Bávaro, Punta Caña and Juanillo. This small town was founded in 1504, and is the religious mecca of the Dominican people. Here is the Basilica of Our Lady of Altagracia, patron saint of the Dominican Republic, whose feast day is January 21.

At **Punta Caña**, the region's very first tourist resort was opened in 1981 by Club Med. Since then, many more facilities have been added along the coast, including four **Bávaro Beach** Resorts, owned by the Barcelo Hotel Company of Spain. These hotels have a total capacity of 1,300 rooms, with access to an 18-hole golf course, casino, and all sport and dining options.

Likewise, the area of **El Macao** is one of the most dynamic tourism development zones of recent years.

With over 20 miles of white sand beach still unexploited, some 3,000 rooms at six new resorts and another 18-hole golf course are expected to come soon into full operation. Still more developments are planned.

5.4 Take a trip

From any of the Caribbean south-coast resorts there is good sightseeing potential in the eastern half of the island. Buses run frequently into Santo Domingo, in addition to regular city tours with a guide.

For other destinations, transport arrangements are not so easy. Car hire is expensive, and renting a motor-scooter can cost you an arm and a leg, with questionable insurance. But local tour companies operate a good range of excursions that pack maximum interest and variety.

As a very approximate price guide, reckon up to US $70 or £47 for long-haul whole-day trips which normally include lunch, open bar and any necessary sport equipment such as a horse or snorkelling gear.

Here are some of the most popular destinations.

Catalina Island
A journey by glass-bottomed boat starts from the mouth of the river Cumayasa near La Romana for a 40-minute ride to Catalina Island, where the white-sand beaches are rated among the best in the Caribbean. The sparkling waters offer good fish-spotting and coral. During the time of Trujillo, the dictator chose the uninhabited $3^1/_2$-square-mile island for one of his house-building projects.

Variations on the Catalina Island theme can include a river trip part-way up the Cumayasa river; or maybe a visit to Altos de Chavón.

Saona Island
Go further along the coastal highway, past La Romana, to embark at Bayahibe Beach on the edge of the National Park of the East, where iguanas still flourish. A 45-minute boat trip cruises past mangrove stands with rich birdlife and possibly sight of dolphins. The National Park also includes Saona Island, which is narrowly separated by the Catuano Channel.

Landing on a white-sand beach, there's a buffet, open bar and time to enjoy the crystal-clear waters. On the south side of Saona Island is a tiny fishing village called Mano Juan, where 300 inhabitants live the simple life, totally innocent of electricity or running water.

Some tour programmes also include a speedboat trip up the Chavón River, which was the film setting for part of the movie *Apocalypse Now*.

Haitises National Park
The route to Haitises Park goes north-east via San Pedro, past sugar cane fields and plantations of cacao and coffee, to reach the southern shore of Samaná Bay. There are no roads within the National Park. From the fishing village of Sabana de la Mar, boats cruise through mangrove swamps that are rich in wildlife. Visitors can see wall paintings and rock carvings in caves formerly inhabited by Taino Indians.

At the orange-grove village of Los Naranjos, there may be time for a refreshing swim in the river. Some excursions stop at a village that specialises in working amber, with the opportunity of buying a piece or two.

Caya Levantado
This trip follows the same route as for Las Haitises National Park, but takes a pleasure cruise from Sabana de la Mar to the so-called Bacardi Island of Caya Levantado. Whale-watching is another option, December until mid-March. See more details on page 29.

Jarabacoa
This beautiful trip features sightseeing of the Central Highlands, possibly with horseback riding through lush countryside and a riverside hike to reach locally famous waterfalls.

Jeep Safari
For a close-up view of the countryside beyond the surfaced highways, try a safari that includes travel by jeep, horse and river boat. Lunch is time for a farm barbecue, with merengue music to accompany those who want to dance. On some tours they even arrange demonstration cock-fights.

Lake Enriquillo
The south-west coast of the Dominican Republic has relatively few facilities, and the access roads are poor. In

Barahona province, beaches are isolated, and have little sand. In this arid and mountainous area is Enriquillo Lake, the largest and lowest in the Antilles, with hypersaline waters that house a very large population of American crocodiles. In the lake are three islands, declared a National Park. On Cabritos island, the crocodiles lay their eggs and spend their nights. Visits to the island are possible with prior permission of the National Parks Bureau.

5.5 *Shopping*

From Boca Chica or Juan Dolio, the widest range of shopping is available in Santo Domingo itself. See the suggested range on page 42.

In Boca Chica itself, a number of galleries and souvenir stores are scattered in the streets that run parallel to the beach.

On excursions to Catalina Island, Altos de Chávon or Saona Island, many tours make a refreshment and giftware halt at the Guina Bamboo Shop, a few miles before reaching La Romana. The gallery displays an unusually wide selection of Dominican-style canvases.

5.6 *Nightlife*

The major hotel-resorts operate their own evening entertainment programmes. From Boca Chica and Juan Dolio, night excursions are made to the capital – see details at the end of the previous chapter. Depending on the package ingredients, a night tour to Santo Domingo could cost around US $25; or up to $40 if dinner is included.

At Boca Chica there's a wide range of casual bars, open-air and disco type, where it's fun to cruise around and meet other holidaymakers and lonesome Dominican girls. In early evening there are Happy Hours with half-price drinks.

Usually there's a once-weekly imitation voodoo show, with barbecue and open bar around a beach bonfire. The performers eat bottles, fire-dance and go into a voodoo trance. Transport to the show can be by minibus, horse or boat, at your choice. Something different again is to go horse riding by moonlight along the beach, with a halt for music, drinking and dancing.

At Juan Dolio there's a casino at Club Decámeron, 20 or 30 minutes by cab from Boca Chica, depending on the machismo of the driver. Reckon a one-way taxi fare of about US $12 or £8.

Chapter Six

The Dominican Republic beyond the beaches

6.1 Basic geography

With a land area of 18,800 square miles, the Dominican Republic is larger than Jamaica and the Bahamas put together. The second biggest Caribbean nation after Cuba, the Republic occupies the eastern two-thirds of the island of Hispaniola, while Haiti takes up the remainder.

Due to its central location, the island was called the "Key to the West Indies" by King Philip II of Spain. Cuba and Jamaica lie to the west; Puerto Rico to the east, beyond the 70-mile Mona Passage. The most southerly tip of Florida is 685 miles away.

Of volcanic origin, the island is split by three mountain chains which create great variety of landscape. There are towering peaks and rocky cliffs, rain forests, fertile valleys and cacti-studded semi-desert. From a thousand miles of coastline, nearly 300 miles are soft sand beaches. The north coast is washed by the Atlantic Ocean; south coast, by the Caribbean Sea.

The highest and lowest points in the Caribbean lie close together in the Dominican Republic. The highest point is 10,414-ft Duarte Peak; the lowest is only 50 miles southwest -Lake Enriquillo, 148 ft below sea level.

The principal mountain range is the Central Cordillera, which runs from Haiti and swings through the central territory to reach south to San Cristobal province, near Santo Domingo.

The Northern Cordillera runs parallel to the Central Range, separating Cibao Valley from the Atlantic coastal plain. Its highest peak is 4,100-ft Diego de Ocampo.

The Eastern Cordillera is the smallest and lowest of the three mountain ranges, stretching along the island's eastern region.

Altogether, 80% of the Dominican Republic is mountainous. Only the south-east is flat. The country has numerous rivers, many of them navigable by small craft.

The prevailing northeast trade winds from the Atlantic are rain-bearing. Because of the mountain layout, the northern coast and mountain slopes have the most rainfall – up to 75" a year – while the southwest corner is arid, with only 12". Likewise there is wide variation in temperature levels between the coast and the mountain peaks.

In turn, these climatic variations lead to great diversity in the country's plants and trees, ranging from thorn forests to mountain conifers. In the northeast coastal areas are enormous palm-groves. Much of the northern region is cattle-ranching country, with lush green meadows. The fertile Cibao Valley supports major production of coffee, tobacco, rice and tropical fruits. The biggest sugar plantations are located in the southeast.

The island is host to innumerable species of tropical birds. Among the rarer animals are manatees and iguanas. There are no major predators, except that Lake Enriquillo is the habitat for one of the world's largest wildlife crocodile populations. Over 10% of the Dominican Republic's territory is protected as National Parks or Scientific Reserves.

The Dominican Republic features two main areas with heavy density of population – Santo Domingo and Santiago. The rest of the country has low average population density.

6.2 The historical background

The past was glorious or grisly, depending on your viewpoint.

Christopher Columbus was the island's first visitor from Europe, arriving on 5th December 1492. Maybe a thousand years earlier, Arawak tribesmen had moved in from South America. They were people of the Taino culture, eating fish, meat, root crops and maize. They spent their considerable spare time relaxing in hammocks, or smoking cigars, drinking alcohol, singing, dancing or playing ball games. Their customs and lifestyle were very close to those of tribesmen today in the Amazon region of Brazil.

The Spanish settlers who arrived in 1493 wanted gold, in addition to drink and women. They brought seeds to plant, but were not interested in field labour. They demanded food and gold from the Indians. When demands were not met, punishment followed. Prisoners became slaves, and the women were used. The first mixed-race children were born.

The original Taino population was an estimated one million. Their numbers fell rapidly, through harsh labour, the import of new European diseases, death as punishment for resistance to slavery, or suicide. Within 15 years their numbers were down to 50,000.

Don Diego, the son of Christopher Columbus, took over as viceroy in 1509. Cultivation of sugar cane had begun, but Diego Columbus faced labour shortage. Taking a census, he found that Taino numbers had faded to 14,000. After a smallpox epidemic in 1518, only 3,000 survived. By 1525 there were none left.

From 1511 onwards, about 5,000 African slaves were imported each year. By law, one-third of the slaves were female, for breeding purposes. As slaves cost money, they were treated less harshly than the Tainos. Spaniards took the more attractive negro girls as concubines, setting the pattern for today's range of skin colours – every shade of brown, from white to black.

This was the basis of the triangular trade: sugar sold to Europe bought consumer goods to trade for West African slaves who were sold in the Caribbean – with big profits along each side of the triangle.

Meanwhile, the Spanish government had written off Hispaniola as a major source of gold. There were much better pickings in South America. Santo Domingo on the southern coast became a base for New World operations, while northern areas of the island became a haven for smugglers, pirates and buccaneers.

Then came the age of Hawkins and his cousin, Drake - pirates according to the Spanish viewpoint – who plundered the Spanish Main, and became the heroes of every English schoolboy. In 1586, Drake captured the capital, Santo Domingo, stayed a month, and ransacked everything before burning the city. In retaliation for Drake's exploits, King Philip of Spain sent the Armada to attack England in 1589. Loss of so many Spanish ships weakened Spain's hold on the Caribbean colonies.

Apart from sugar plantations in the south, and cattle ranches in the north, Hispaniola was de-populated in the countryside. By mid-17th century, the white population was around 15,000, with perhaps 150,000 black and mixed – far fewer than the original population of Tainos. In 1655 Cromwell ordered an English fleet to capture the island, but the campaign was a disaster. The force retreated, and captured Jamaica instead.

Meanwhile the French were targeting the island, with settlers moving into the west and the northwest. Some kind of local balance was achieved, recognised in 1678 by the Nimega peace treaty between Spain and France.

French colonists concentrated on sugar plantations, based on intensive black slave labour. Spanish ranchers specialised in hides and foodstuffs. Island trade blossomed between the French plantation economy in the west, and the Spanish in the east. The lines were set for the division of Hispaniola. In 1697 the Treaty of Ryswick formally recognised the split between Spanish and French spheres of influence – though not until 1776 was there firm agreement on the exact boundary that still divides the island between the Dominican Republic and Haiti.

By the early 18th century, the dual economy had prospered, thanks to Europe's high demand for sugar. Spain tried to build up strength in Hispaniola by encouraging migrants from the Canary Islands. France expanded plantations through importation of still more slaves. By the late 18th century, Haiti had over 500,000 inhabitants, mainly blacks in sugar trade. The Dominican Republic had barely 100,000 people, in ranching, tobacco and coffee.

In the shake-up of the French Revolution, black revolt was inevitable. Slavery was abolished in Haiti in 1793. In 1795 the entire island came under French rule. Armies marched back and forth across the island in conflicts between French and Spanish and blacks and mulattoes. There were rebellions, and generals switched sides. Dominican slaves were freed when a Haitian army led by the negro general Toussaint invaded the Spanish side in 1801.

Then Napoleon's men under General Leclerc regained control of the island in 1802, Toussaint was outlawed, captured and sent to prison in France where he soon died. Slavery was re-established. The mulattoes and blacks rebelled again. Dessalines, commander of the negroes, forced a French surrender in 1803. He proclaimed himself Emperor of Haiti on January 1st 1804, and slaves were again freed. He was a brutal and bloodthirsty man, setting the pattern for future Haitian despots.

On the Spanish side of the island, French and Spanish troops clashed, with the British navy helping to oust the French in 1809. The British did not leave until their campaign expenses had been paid. Slavery was re-introduced. The end result of all these years of confusion was bankruptcy. That was followed by the so-called Era of Foolish Spain, when the parent government showed little interest in its colony.

Amid more turmoil of plots and counter-plots, the Dominicans in 1821 proclaimed the birth of the Independent State of Spanish Haiti. But this independence lasted only a few weeks. Haitian troops marched in and took over the whole island, claiming that "the island is one and indivisible and should therefore not have two governments".

Slavery was again abolished, but plantation workers had to stay put on wages. A rural code to break up ranches for individual farming was an economic failure, with neglect of cash crops in favour of subsistence agriculture.

Finally, after years of plotting, Haitian occupation was ended in 1844 and the Dominican Republic proclaimed. The three leaders, whose names are still honoured, were Duarte, Sánchez and Mella. However, a military coup installed General Santana as President, and the three 'fathers of the nation' were imprisoned and then expelled for life.

So the 19th century passed in move and counter-move. In 1861 the Republic was re-annexed to Spain. But Spanish troops were felled in great numbers by yellow fever, to which the locals were acclimatized. Only 300 survived from a force of 5,000. In 1864 another 20,000 Spanish troops were poured in, and promptly went down with fever. After a few more battles, the Spanish gave up, and the Republic was Restored.

But the economy remained a mess. With the second Republic came a series of civil wars followed by democratic governments. Big international loans were raised at high interest, and American gunboats arrived to ensure stability. In 1871 there were plans to annex the Dominican Republic to USA, but the schemes fell through.

In 1905, the United States took partial control of the Dominican economy to protect American investors. By 1916 the problem of increasing national debts and internal disorders led to occupation by U.S. Marines.

American occupation with military government lasted until 1924, bringing relative prosperity through easy sale of cash crops – sugar, coffee, tobacco, rice – to the wide-open US market. The Dominicans learned to love baseball.

The third republic lasted from 1924 till 1965. But 31 of those years were under the dictatorship of General Rafael Trujillo, from 1930 until 1961. History gives a thumbs-down verdict on Trujillo, who ruled with brutality. Civil rights were ignored, and secret police made arrests unchallenged. In a burst of ethnic cleansing, 25,000 Haitian immigrants were slaughtered in 1937. Trujillo became one of the world's richest men, milking the country's economy for himself, his favourite mistress and his cronies. Opposition grew, and the Organization of American States voted to ostracize him.

Trujillo was assassinated in 1961 by army leaders, and democracy was more or less restored. In December 1962 free elections gave the presidency to left-wing Juan Bosch. His reform programme led to a military coup nine months later.

In 1965 civil war broke out, to be extinguished by the landing of 30,000 US Marines to prevent the Republic from going the way of Cuba. Between April and September 1965 the country had seven different administrations. Peace-keeping troops from the Organization of American States remained until order was restored in 1966. Since then, elections have been held every four years, in line with the constitution.

6.3 *The economy*

The mainstays of the Dominican economy are agriculture and agro-industry, mining, tourism, and industrial free zones.

Formerly dependent on export of raw materials, the country has been transformed to a service supplier. The most dynamic sector is tourism, followed by light manufacturing especially in the industrial free zones. Tourism has been the biggest foreign income earner since 1984. But traditional agriculture and mining still contribute to the nation's economy. Farming accounts for 15% of Gross Domestic Product and employs 49% of the labour force.

The main export crops are: sugar followed by coffee, cotton, cocoa, and tobacco. Other exportable crops are bananas, pineapples, oranges, flowers and vegetables.

Mining is concentrated mainly in the Cibao region, which has deposits of ferro-nickel, bauxite, copper, marble, rock salt and gypsum. The government-owned Rosario open-cast gold mine is claimed to be the largest in the western hemisphere.

Major industries in the Free Zones are clothing, footwear, furniture, electronics, sporting goods, pharmaceuticals, data entry and other service operations. Outside of Free Zones, products manufactured for export are canned and processed fruits and vegetables and cocoa butter. Major non-food exports are clothing, wood furniture and batteries.

6.4 Cash crops and fruit

For garden-lovers there's great pleasure in touring through the countryside, and seeing first-hand how the tropical crops, fruits and vegetables are grown.

Major plantation crops are sugar cane, coffee, cocoa, tobacco, rice, coconuts, pineapples and bananas. Smaller farms and backyard plots produce maize, beans, onions, sweet potatoes and other tubers for domestic consumption and local market sale. But land is being reallocated for increased production of non-traditional export crops such as winter vegetables and exotic fruits. You can see avocado trees, mangoes, papayas, passion fruit, citrus, peanuts and cashews.

Here are some background notes.

Sugar

Ever since Christopher Columbus brought sugar cane to the island in 1493, sugar has played a dominant role in the economy. For centuries there was fast-expanding world demand for the end product, bringing riches to estate owners. The annual consumption of sugar in Europe rose from 2 kgs per person in 1700 to more than 40 kgs in the 1930's. Today there are Government-owned plantations in Puerto Plata province. But the biggest estates are in the south-east.

Sugar cane is harvested once a year, usually starting around mid-May when the cane is anything from 4 to 10 feet tall. Cutting is done by hand, with machetes, no machinery.

It's very tough labour-intensive work – so hard and poorly paid that few Dominican citizens want to know. Hence the presence of immigrant Haitian cane-cutters.

When the cane is cut, new shoots arise from the stubble, growing up ready for next year.

The Dominican Republic has 17 mills which process the cane. Of the total sugar production, 75% is exported. A by-product is molasses, which is fermented to meet local demand for rum, of which only 5% is left for export.

Bananas

Shortly after the arrival of Columbus, banana trees were introduced from the Canary Islands into Hispaniola. From there, the trees spread throughout the Caribbean and to Central and South America – to all the latter-day banana republics.

A banana plantation provides year-round fruit. In the Dominican Republic, the best bananas, large and sweet, come from Monte Cristi province. But bananas grow well, almost anywhere in the island – also as a backyard crop for domestic consumption. A close relative is the plantain, looking like a large green banana, and cooked as a vegetable. Banana exports go mostly to USA, but also to Britain.

The plant is hermaphrodite: male and female flowers on the same stalk. Reproduction takes place without pollination. The first flowers appear when the plant is about one year old. Bananas are the female part of the flower, and at the tip of the flower stalk is the male organ. Each row of bananas is separated by large purple bracts, or petals, which are cut off by hand to expose the bananas to the sun.

The bananas gradually turn upwards, and fatten. The stem is cut green for export at six or seven months. After removal of the fruit, the thick fibrous stems are used as fodder. The original plant dies, but is replaced by suckers.

Coconuts

Millions of coconut palms flourish in coastal areas, with the greatest concentration on the Samaná Peninsula. The tree is cultivated mainly for oil extracted from the dried copra. Crude oil is an ingredient in soap and cosmetics, while refined oil is used for cooking, and for manufacture of margarine and salad oils. Coconut milk can double as a suntan lotion, and plays a key role in piño coladas.

Wayside vendors offer fresh coconut milk, scalping the fruit with a machete. Dominicans claim that coconut juice is an aphrodisiac, though that may be just a sales pitch. People who stop for a drink also own the flesh of the coconut. But usually they don't bother, just leaving it with the street vendor.

By-products help rank the coconut palm among the world's most useful trees. The outer casing makes good fertilizer, while the very strong coir fibre is used for rope-making, coarse brushes and matting. The second shell burns well as fuel. Palm leaves make an economy thatch.

Coconuts are disseminated by independent sea travel. The fibrous husk keeps the fruit afloat, while the tough skin prevents water-logging. Swept by tides and currents onto a distant shore, the nut germinates rapidly, even after four months' afloat.

Growing 100 feet tall, coconut palms begin to yield after six years, and remain productive for a century. If a fruit is harvested green from four months onwards, it contains mostly sweet milk. Otherwise the fruit takes a year to ripen, when the milk has become solid and oily to produce the coconut meat. An average tree bears over 40 nuts annually, yielding about 20 lbs of copra from which a gallon of oil can be extracted.

Rice

In the Cibao valley – near Santiago, for instance – rice paddies add brilliant green to the landscape. You can see all stages of rice growing, with farm workers squelching ankle deep in oozing mud to plant seedlings. Enough rice is produced for domestic needs, leaving a surplus for export.

Tobacco

The Taino Indians cultivated tobacco long before Columbus arrived, and smoked it in cigar style mixed with narcotic herbs. Certainly it was on Hispaniola that Europeans first encountered the noxious weed. Even the use of snuff was first observed here.

Cultivation today is mainly in the Cibao Valley – cigar filler types which are exported to USA as a substitute for banned Cuban tobacco. A thriving industry is located in Santiago. Factories welcome visitors to watch the making of hand-rolled cigars which can rival Havanas.

Coffee

Dominicans are addicted to their locally-grown coffee, which is cultivated in highland areas around Moca, and also near Bani in Peravia Province in the south. Dominican coffee has a good reputation on export markets, but is less profitable owing to a world glut. Major brands to take home for coffee-loving friends are Cafe Santo Domingo, La Tacita, and Cafe Puro – available at most supermarkets.

The coffee tree is an evergreen some 12 feet high, with glistening dark green leaves. The tiny berries are harvested in the autumn, about 1000 seeds to a pound.

Cacao

The cacao tree produces the totally different bean from which cocoa and chocolate are made. Widely grown along the Río Yaqui valley, the 25-ft evergreen trees produce large red pods, each containing about 50 bitter-tasting beans. These seeds, weighing about 200 to the pound, are dried in the sun for three days. Then they are roasted and ground for cocoa and chocolate manufacture.

Chapter Seven

Shopping

A favourable exchange rate ensures bargain shopping for colourful handicrafts and other local products. Most popular are jewellery designs made from amber or larimar semi-precious stone, wicker, rattan and wood furniture, hand-painted masks, macramé, ceramics, straw and woven goods, carved mahogany sculptures, Dominican fine art and paintings, fashions from local-born designers, rum and cigars.

Santo Domingo has large commercial malls, while smaller shopping centres are found in other cities. Store hours follow the lunchtime siesta tradition: 8-12 and 14-18 hrs Mondays to Saturdays. Supermarkets are open from 8-20 hrs Mon-Sat with no lunchtime closure.

The public market and beachside outlets are the most fun when looking for handicrafts. In these locations, haggling is expected. Opening prices are pitched so that you can enjoy beating them down.

Similar products in hotel boutiques are often better quality at a higher fixed price.

Duty free shopping is available at Las Américas and Puerto Plata Airports, but with no great bargains. Items like rum and cigars are cheaper in ordinary town shops, or bought when you visit the bottling plant or factory.

Colmados are neighbourhood convenience stores, open whenever people are most likely to buy, including Sundays. In the countryside they also double as bars, and stay open till late.

Post offices are open Mon-Fri 8-17 hrs, Sat 8-14 hrs. Air mail to UK costs 3 pesos, but can take weeks to arrive.

What to buy

Amber is a golden resin, hardened like stone during 30 to 50 million years of fossilization. The world's richest deposits are found in northern areas of the Dominican Republic. Hence the popular name of the Atlantic shoreline: the Amber Coast.

Colour of the fossilized wood resin varies mainly from yellow to golden chestnut, but the full range includes white, lemon, amarillo, maroon, green, red, black, opaque and – the rarest – blue. Neither of the two other major amber producing countries – Germany and Russia – can match the colours and clarity of Dominican amber. The clearer the stone, the higher the value for gems which are polished, and made into attractive jewellery. Caution: some cheap 'amber' is plastic – unsaturated polyester, the stuff used to repair fibreglass boats. Earlier fakes were made of Bakelite. It's hard for the non-specialist to tell the difference.

An interesting Amber Museum in Puerto Plata has an authentic selection on display. Some specimens contain volcanic ash, ancient plants, insects and even a small lizard.

Larimar has been recognised since 1974 as a semi-precious gemstone, found only in the Dominican Republic. Described as the 'Dominican turquoise', it is often mounted in silver or gold settings, to make attractive jewellery: rings, bracelets, earrings and necklaces. The blue colour derives from the presence of cobalt oxide during the stone's geological formation. The deeper blue shades are made into gold trinkets; and the lighter blue set in silver. Larimar has now been honoured as the national stone of the Dominican Republic.

Black coral is ripped from the reefs and converted into items of souvenir jewellery. If visitors stopped buying it, the damaged coral reefs could have a better chance of survival. A good substitute is made of cow horn or plastic, and most people cannot tell the difference except for the lower price. Buy the cow horn imitation, and give yourself Brownie points for helping to preserve the environment.

Paintings are everywhere, in the primitive Haitian style of riotous colour. Beach markets display them by the acre, production-line canvasses all done by hand. Copy after copy is produced, with the same basic theme: waving palm-trees beside a golden beach; girl with bananas on her head; a swirling array of coloured circles; hundreds of heads, jostled in a crowd. Once an artist has found his theme, he stays with it for life. There's always another buyer at around £10 upwards.

Pottery On some excursions to Santiago, retail outlets give a standard pottery tour, demonstrating a kick-wheel for production of well-crafted pots. Hundreds of traditional dolls with unpainted faces are on display, both in pottery and textile; and devil masks as used in some of Santiago's festivals. Many of the very decorative pottery souvenirs are copies of Taino artefacts that were produced before the Spaniards arrived.

Cigars are locally produced, and can make a dedicated smoker very happy. The top-grade hand-rolled cigars can match the quality of a good Havana. Large numbers are exported to USA, which has a political ban on all Cuban products. Effectively the Dominican Republic has captured the American market for highest-quality cigars.

Chapter Eight

Eating and drinking

The major hotels and restaurants concentrate on standard international cuisine. But mostly they also provide a daily selection of local dishes. Traditional Dominican cuisine is worth trying. It's a mixture of the ethnic influences that have created a national identity: a savoury yet subtle blend of native Indian, Spanish and African ingredients.

You can sample some of these specialities at hotel buffet meals, where a label with local or Spanish name – usually with English translation – is attached to each food item on display.

Typical dishes are:

Asopao – a rice soup with meat or fish

La Bandera Dominicana – Rice and beans and meat. Red beans are prepared in a tomato and onion sauce, while the rice is cooked separately. Then they put the two together, with any type of meat. Just ask for **una bandera**.

Casabe – the flat Indian cassava bread, a crispy type of pizza bread. In the resort areas, garlic is often added.

Catibias – cassava or manioc fritters stuffed with meat.

Chicharrón – fried crispy pork crackling, bought at roadside stands. The grease rolls down your arms to your elbows, and it's delicious, even if the hygienic standards are dubious. The meat itself is sold separately.

Chicharrones de pollo – small pieces of deep-fried chicken with batter

Chivo Guisado – tasty stewed or oven-baked goat.

Chorizo – beef sausage

Congrí – featured at a Dominican buffet at some hotels: a spit-roasted pig stuffed with rice and black beans.

Fish in Coconut Sauce – a favourite of the northeast coast.

Fritos Verdes (or tostones) – fried slices of green bananas - plantains. Served instead of **Papas fritas** – French fries.

Lambí – conch

Lechon asado – roast pork

Locrio – a meat and vegetable stew, with a rice base: an adaptation of the Spanish paella.

Longaniza – a spiced pork sausage

Mangú – mashed plantains, fried with egg or onions, and often served at breakfast.

Mondongo – a tripe soup

Morcilla – a blood sausage

Moro – a dry fried mixture of rice and beans or peas

Pasteles en Hojas – plantain-dough boiled meat pies wrapped in banana leaves

Salsa criolla – a Creole sauce based mainly on tomato and coconuts.

Sancocho – A Dominican stew with everything: a gravy base, varied assortment of vegetables like potatoes or yucca, and an assortment of meat – chicken, pork, beef. But the real version also has duck, goat, sausage, with some white rice applied separately. Other vegetables can be squash, carrots or plantain, and pumpkin as a colouring. In the countryside they also add bitter orange.

Stewed Goat – one of the favourite rural specialities

Tostones – fried plantain – green bananas used as a vegetable, cooked. Not for eating raw!

All the fruits

Thanks to the Dominican Republic's wide range of climatic zones, the country harvests a year-round choice of tropical fruits. Bananas, pineapples, coconuts, melons and watermelons, oranges, lemons, grapefruit, mangoes and limes are familiar enough. But there are many other fruits which are more difficult to recognise by visitors from North America or Europe.

Especially delicious is passion fruit (*chinola*), which makes an excellent drink or is superb with a scrape of honey. Papaya (*lechosa*) is a good breakfast starter, with a twitch of lemon or lime juice to enliven its otherwise bland flavour. Guava (*guayaba*) provides excellent fruit juice, and can be converted into marmelade. Sapodilla (*zapote*) is a rough-skinned fruit like a plum, used in ice cream and milk shakes.

Among other fruits that appear in farmers' markets are tamarind (*tamarindo*), medlar (*níspero*), and custard apple (*guanábana*). Another fruit worth trying is the *mamey* – size of a grapefruit with red skin and yellow pulp.

Desserts

If you have a sweet tooth, the Dominican Republic is paradise. The main purpose of confectioners is to support the local sugar industry. Cakes and puddings are always extremely sweet.

Rum cocktails
Caribbean ingenuity has devised many ways of absorbing the fruit, sugar and rum mountains.

Here are some popular variations.

Piña Colada – white rum, pineapple juice, lemon juice, coconut and ice.

Coco loco – a crazy coconut – is the same as a piña colada but without the pineapple juice.

Banana Mama – like piña colada, but with grenadine.

Rum punch – rum, lemon juice, sugar, soda water and ice.

Fruit punch – rum, different fruit juices, soda and ice (also possible without the rum).

Daiquiri – white rum, lemon juice, sugar and ice.

Banana-daiquiri – as for daiquiri, but with banana and orange juice.

Rum cocktail – rum, gin, lemon juice, sugar and ice.

Merengue cocktail – rum, orange juice, lemon juice, apricot brandy and sugar.

Cuba libre – a famous calypso gives you the ingredients: rum and Coca-Cola.

Rum is not clobbered by taxation, and is therefore very cheap. If you're visiting a bottling plant, an average rum costs under £2 sterling or three US dollars. Supermarket prices aren't much more, but hotel mini-markets could charge double.

Three leading brands of rum begin with 'B' – Brugal, bottled in Puerto Plata; Bermudez in Santiago; Barceló in Santo Domingo. A fourth major brand is Macorís, bottled in San Pedro de Macorís.

As a heart-warming souvenir to remind you of Caribbean sunshine, consider buying a higher-priced but well-aged rum - 10 or 12 years' old – which is good to drink straight.

The rum of 151 proof – popularly known as Gasoline – is virtually pure alcohol, and is like being shot in the throat if taken neat. But it's the preferred rum for making cocktails such as piña colada.

National brands of beer: Presidente, Quisqueya and Bohemia. All are light Pilsener-type bottled beers, served very cold.

Wines: The Dominican Republic produces small quantities of local wine, but most of the ordinary table wine is imported from Chile or Spain. Quality European wines and champagnes are sold only in top-grade restaurants and – to the distress of wine-lovers – are astronomically expensive.

Chapter Nine

Transport

The Dominican Republic has five international airports, with another under construction. Only two receive scheduled international flights – Las Américas airport near Santo Domingo, serving the island's southern shore; and Puerto Plata, feeding the north coast resorts. The other three airports are limited to small aircraft and charter flights.

Highways

Travelling around locally can give you a colourful insight into the Dominican way of life. Three major trunk roads link the capital city of Santo Domingo to the regions. Of most importance is the Duarte Highway which runs from the north-western corner of the island – at Monte Cristi, near the Haitian border – towards Puerto Plata and via Santiago to the capital. The Sénchez Highway goes south and then west from Santo Domingo, while the Mella Highway leads towards the south-eastern corner of the island.

Altogether, the Dominican Republic can boast of around 12,000 miles of highways and secondary roads. But standards are Latin American, not European or North American. Only one third of the network is metalled, and even heavy trucks prefer to weave around the pot-holes.

Driving is on the right. Speed limits are 80 kilometres per hour on highways, 60 kph in suburban areas, and 40 kph in cities, unless otherwise specified on traffic signs. Traffic theoretically overtakes on the left, but don't depend on it. Drivers often cut through on the right, especially when slow-moving vehicles hug the middle of the road. Beating the red light is a favourite macho sport.

Car and motor-bike rental

A valid driver's license and major credit card are required to rent a car. Tariffs are much higher than in Europe or North America, mainly because very high import duties make cars very costly to buy. Many companies require minimum two-day rental for unlimited mileage. Single day renters pay additional per mile.

Deterred by the elevated car-rental tariffs, some visitors hire a motor-cycle or scooter for 200 or 300 pesos a day. If you are tempted, carefully check on insurance. You may find there's no cover either for accident or theft. The form that you sign may indicate that you are personally responsible if the vehicle is damaged or stolen.

Because of the bad roads and poor road discipline, motorcycle or scooter hire is not recommended. Accidents are frequent, and it's unlikely that you'll be supplied with a helmet.

If your hired bike disappears, you are liable to pay the full value of the loss. Because of import costs, the bill will be far higher than in Britain. There has even been suspicion that the owner himself has 'stolen' the vehicle, and demanded full payment for replacement. It's a very tricky area. Be on your guard.

Public transport

Taxis – For local transport, the easiest option is the taxi rank at the hotel entrance. A board displays fixed tariffs, which are not negotiable. Hotel taxis are much more costly than other forms of transport. But they are mostly large and elderly American-made cars which can take four or six passengers. The shared cost is then not so painful.

If a return trip is required, the driver charges double the single fare, with an agreed waiting time included; or he returns at an agreed pick-up time. To ensure you are not left stranded, the cabbie is not paid until completion of the return trip. If you take a taxi where the fares are not displayed, agree a price before starting your journey.

Other options are much cheaper. Wander out to the main road, and survey the passing transport: buses, minibuses, public cars and *moto-concho* motorbike taxis. Let's look closer. **Local buses** are not the most sedate form of travel but they are cheap – Sosúa to Puerto Plata costs approx 50p, Playa Dorada to Puerto Plata about 10p. Some offer reasonable comfort; others don't.

Short-distance minibuses are known as *guaguas* (pronounced wah-wah). It's like travelling in a rusty sardine can. Designed with about 15 seats, capacity can be doubled by use of jump seats, sitting on friendly knees, and half-crouching on the floor. The last few passengers and the conductor hang on by their finger-tips outside the open door.

Guaguas are the general means of transport from town to town, and stop anywhere on request. Fares vary from 2 to 20 pesos, depending on the distance. Keep small change handy in order to pay the exact fare. Otherwise, as a rich foreigner, you'll pay over the odds.

Carros publicos are the most common mode of transportation in the cities: small saloon cars operating along set routes at one standard fare. They normally carry a human cargo of about 50% more than the designer ever imagined in his worst nightmares. Public cars – also known as Concho Cars – can also be hired for your exclusive use, like a taxi. This contract is called a *carrera*. Agree the fare before using the service.

Moto-conchos are 50-cc Hondas or 100-cc Yamahas which offer a popular and very cheap form of transport among the locals. The passenger rides pillion – sometimes several passengers, like a woman with two children. Nobody wears a helmet. The ride can be very bumpy, with sudden swerves whenever cross-traffic doesn't adhere to standard rules about priority. It's rather like Russian Roulette on wheels, not recommended. At a typical moto-concho stand, up to twenty riders are lined up for customers, all ready to zoom off. These city cowboys have given up horses, and now ride motor-bikes in the same John Wayne spirit.

Inter-city buses – Finally, some transport which can be recommended. An excellent bus system provides scheduled transport between Santo Domingo and major cities.

Metro and Caribe Tours are the two main bus lines that operate several times daily between Puerto Plata and Santo Domingo in 4 hours, via Santiago: fare around £4 or US$ 6. The Metro buses call themselves Air Bus – nothing to do with flight, but air conditioned. Lower-fare buses also cover the same routes, but these can be very overcrowded.

Metro's system is that you make a reservation by phone, and are given a number. Pick up your ticket at the bus station at least half an hour before departure. After that deadline, they may not hold your reservation, but sell your seat to anyone else.

The 54-seater bus is built like an American Greyhound with reclining seats, footrests, tinted windows, curtains and good leg-room. It's a comfortable ride, very punctual, no smoking, and no talking to the driver.

During the journey the conductor offers small packets of free biscuits, cakes or nuts. Latin American music plays all the way, but at tolerable volume – though maybe that depends on the driver's preference. A 10-minute rest stop at Santiago features adequate WC's.

Chapter Ten

Learn some Spanish

Spanish is the official language of the Dominican Republic, though most people connected with tourism have enough English for their job. However, there's pleasure in being able to use and recognise even just a few words of Spanish. Some club resorts include a basic daily lesson in their activities programme – a kind of mental aerobics.

Your waiter's usual friendly greeting is "Hola amigo!", or "Hola papa!" or "Hola mama!" if you have a trace of grey hair. It's nice to make the same response, or beat him to it.

Certainly some Spanish is helpful when venturing beyond your resort. If you are self-driving or exploring in more off-trail areas, it's useful to carry a pocket phrase-book.

If you already know Spanish, be prepared for a few adjustments. In mainland Spain, 'c' before 'i' or 'e' is pronounced like 'th' in 'think'; likewise for 'z'. But in Latin America, 'c' and 'z' are variants of 's'.

Also, many Latin American words are quite different from European Spanish. The proximity of the Dominican Republic to USA has even introduced North Americanisms into the local language. After you've gone to the trouble of learning that 'goodbye' is *adiós*, it's maddening to find that Dominicans usually say 'bye-bye'. A car is *un carro*.

A few Taino words have survived into the 20th century. Indeed, some of the words used by the original inhabitants have become totally international: *barbacoa* – barbecue; *canoe* – canoe; *caribe* – Caribbean; *casabe* – cassava; *guayaba* – guava; *hamaca* – hammock; *huracán* – hurricane; *iguana* – iguana; *maíz* – maize; *tabaco* – tobacco; *yuca* - yucca (manioc root).

Don't worry about the accents. Apart from ñ (pronounced as in onion), the accents merely indicate the syllable to stress. Otherwise they don't change the vowel sound.

For the beginner in Dominican Spanish, here's a starter kit of a few words to show you're trying.

Greetings

Hello	hola
Goodbye	bye-bye
Good morning	buenos dias
Good afternoon	buenas tardes
Good evening	buenas noches
How are you?	¿cómo está usted?
Very well, thank you	muy bien, gracias

General

Yes	sí
No	no
Please	por favor
Thank you	gracias
Do you speak English?	¿habla inglés?
I don't understand	no comprendo
What time is it?	¿qué hora es?

Shopping

Bank	banco
Currency exchange	cambio
Chemist	farmacia
Doctor	médico
Hairdresser	peluqueria
Supermarket	supermercado
Tobacconist	estanco
Post office	correos
Stamps	sellos
Postcard	postal
How much is it?	¿cuanto es?

Signs

Abierto	open
Ascensor	lift/elevator
Baño damas	ladies' WC
Baño hombres	gents WC
Caliente	hot
Cerrado	shut
Empujar	push
Entrada	entrance
Frío	cold
Libre	vacant
Ocupado	occupied
Parada de autobús	bus stop
Parada de taxis	cab rank
Prohibido entrar	no entrance
Prohibido fumar	no smoking
Salida	exit
Salida de emergencia	emergency exit
Tirar	pull

Numbers

0	cero
1-10	uno, dos, tres, cuatro, cinco, seis, siete, ocho, nueve, diez.
11-19	once, doce, trece, catorce, quince, dieciseis, diecisiete, dieciocho, diecinueve
20-29	veinte, veintiuno, veintidos, veintetres etc.
30-39	treinta, treinta y uno, treinta y dos, etc.
40, 50 -90	cuaranta, cincuenta, sesenta, setenta, ochenta, noventa
100	cien/ciento
101	ciento uno
200	doscientos
500	quinientos
1000	mil
2000	dos mil
1,000,000	un millón

Sightseeing

Where is …?	¿ Donde esta… ?
the beach	la playa
the church	la iglesia
the museum	el museo
the port	el puerto
the square	la plaza
the station	la estación
the street	la calle
the seafront promenade	el malecón

Chapter Eleven

Travel tips and information

11.1 Entertainment & Nightlife

Most of the all-inclusive resort hotels feature their own programmes of daytime and evening entertainment. Typically a house band plays from 8.30 to 9.30 p.m. That may be followed by a light-hearted mini-contest for 15 minutes – anything from best sunburn to pitching ping-pong balls into pots.

Then it's showtime with professional performers mostly from the Dominican Republic, but also from other Caribbean islands. When that's over, disco time starts – continuing as long as demand holds out. Usually, at hotel discos, the entrance price includes any local drink. At discos frequented by Dominicans the custom is to order a "Servicio": a bottle of rum and a supply of soda or Coke.

Merengue

On the popular music scene, you'll soon discover that the Dominicans are mad about merengue – the dance form that is equally popular in neighbouring Haiti. Generally the two countries have kept relatively few cultural links. The exception is in music and folklore, with common roots that go back 200 years.

Merengue is a very lively Caribbean dance that stems both from tribal West Africa and courtly Europe. With their mixed African and Spanish heritage, the local Dominicans have rhythm in their genes. Merengue is similar to the Brazilian samba and lambada. Most hotels include lessons in their entertainment programmes. If you like to swing your hips, you'll have no problem in getting your merengue certificate.

A basic merengue group comprises three instruments: a small drum called a *tambora*, a squeeze-box accordion called a melodeon, and a metal-scraper instrument called *güiro* which comes in different shapes. Some could double as a kitchen cheese-grater. The beat is fast, and the words are humorous or satirical.

Wander along any Dominican street, and you'll hear merengue music played full blast from around dawn till midnight. Settle down to a peaceful siesta on a beach, and three folk minstrels will give a personalized performance until you bribe them to move on. If you want to recapture the mood back home, there are innumerable cassettes and CD's on the market. Top names to seek are Johnny Ventura, Wilfredo Vargas and Jean Luís Guerra.

Casinos

Around 15 hotels in the Republic operate gambling casinos in Las Vegas style, featuring blackjack, craps, roulette, slot machines, poker and baccarat. Casinos are open 4 p.m. to 4 a.m. – weekends until 6 a.m. Players must be over 18 years' old.

These casinos are big business. Roulette is played on American rules with a double zero, which loads the odds in the bank's favour. The house scoops everything twice in 38 spins of the wheel, against once in 37 times with European roulette.

For blackjack – also known as pontoon or twentyone – the dealer must twist on 16, but stick on 17.

The slots are either of the totally mechanical type where you pull the handle and the machine pays out or stays silent. The other slots, especially those based on some variation of poker, demand some mental input from the player.

Electronic poker has a basic resemblance to the card game played by human beings. But you'll probably need some friendly guidance to understand each machine, which have different rules, one to another. Some pay out on pairs or three-of-a-kind; others don't, but compensate by introducing wild cards into the game.

The learning process needn't cost you more than fun money. A typical machine operates with tokens worth 25 US cents. You can bet up to five tokens for each electronic deal. From the cashier you buy a roll or two of 25-cent pieces, handily wrapped in bundles of forty for ten US dollars. At the gaming tables, you buy chips right there from the croupier. Anyone who is actively playing the tables or the slots is plied with free drink.

Voodoo

There are voodoo shows as a tourist entertainment, but authentic voodoo is beyond reach of the average visitor. It's an African cult that survives mainly in Haiti, and to a limited extent in remote areas of the Dominican Republic. Voodoo rites date from the import of slaves during the 17th century. The cult deities are related to African gods, or to the spirits of dead ancestors, or to the spirits of fire, water or wind.

During a terrifying ritual, a devotee enters into a trance, and a spirit takes control of his body. Possessed by this inner demon, the individual assumes a totally different personality. Snakes, graveyards, coffins, shrouds, bones and skulls highlight the cult symbolism. Voodoo priests are especially feared for their reputed power to create a zombie: a corpse that is reanimated and possessed by a spirit under his command.

Travel agencies offer several variations on voodoo evenings: around a camp fire, possibly in a beachside or a riverside setting. Drums, dancing and devil masks provide plentiful subjects for dramatic flash pictures.

11.2 Sport

From ping-pong to polo, there's chance of playing or watching most international sports, but not cricket. Although most equipment is available free or for hire, you may prefer to bring your own tennis racket or snorkel, flippers and mask; and a hard hat if you intend to go horse-riding.

Water-sports – The Amber Coast is ideal for all water sports. Cabarete Beach is rated among the world's top windsurfing spots. Everywhere there are magnificent locations for deep sea fishing, snorkelling and scuba diving.

In many of the hotel resorts, a selection of water sports is included at no extra charge. Otherwise, here are some approximate prices in sterling: windsurfing, sailing dinghy, pedaloes – £11 per hour; jet skis £13 for 15 minutes; waterskiing £13 for 20 minutes; parasailing £23 a go; banana ride, £4 for 15 minutes; scuba diving £250 for a 4-day PADI course; deep sea fishing, £50 for 5 hours including beer.

Golf – There are several excellent golf courses – the best at Casa de Campo and in Playa Dorada. At Playa Dorada's 18-hole Robert Trent Jones Golf Course, green fees are £13, caddies £5 and carts £12. The Costambar golf course has 9 holes, with green fees at £7, caddies £2.50 and carts £6.

Baseball – Among the spectator sports, baseball heads the list. This national sport is played year-round on both an amateur and professional level. There is a summer and a winter league, though the latter is higher rated with six professional teams competing for championship. The top teams are in San Pedro de Macorís, La Romana, Santiago, Puerto Plata, and two in Santo Domingo. They play each other during the winter season, October to January. Then the winners tour other Caribbean destinations such as Puerto Rico, Venezuela and Mexico. This decides which team is the Caribbean champion.

The players' dream is to migrate to the big money in USA. The Dominican Republic outnumbers all other Latin American nations with the most ballplayers – 50 – playing in the North American Major League.

Besides baseball, other popular spectator sports are Basketball, Soft Ball and Volley Ball.

Cock-fighting is not the prettiest of spectator sports, and a visit to a cock-fight is not recommended. But it's wildly popular among Dominicans who want to feel macho and virile.

These events are held mostly on Sundays in pits known as "Galleras". All rural communities, and most cities, have cockpits where matches can be watched amid scenes of gambling bedlam.

On some excursions into the country, there's the possibility of seeing how fighting cocks are trained and prepared for their blood-soaked battles. A demonstration fight can be staged without using the lethal razor-sharp spurs.

11.3 *Tipping*

Hotels and restaurants add an obligatory 10% service charge plus 8% sales tax to mealtime bills. It is customary to give perhaps an additional 5% if you think the waiter deserves it. Porters would hope to receive ten pesos for luggage. Maids are tipped according to service.

For taxi drivers, no extra tipping is necessary, as foreign visitors are anyway paying more than the locals. On excursions, guides and drivers don't expect anything, but a 10- or 20-peso note is appreciated if they have performed well.

11.4 *Electricity*

The current is 110 volts, 60 cycles. Any gadgets you bring must be switcheable to that voltage. You should also take an adaptor, as the Dominican Republic uses flat two-pin American style plugs.

Power cuts are frequent. As a matter of government policy, engineers give VIP priority to restoring power to holiday resorts. But ordinary Dominicans aren't so lucky. However, most hotels have an emergency generator which comes into operation a few minutes after a power failure.

11.5 *Time*

The Dominican Republic is 4 hours behind GMT, and doesn't alter clocks for summer. Thus, during Britain's 'summer time', the Dominican Republic is 5 hours behind UK; or the same as Eastern Standard Time of New York and Miami.

Attitudes towards time are Latin. 'Immediately' translates as *mañana*. The Spanish siesta is normal. After the midday meal, it's heads down for an hour's nap, sleeping or dozing in a chair, or even stretched out on the ground or in a hammock. Siesta time is from 12 to 14 hrs, which is rather different from Mediterranean siesta hours.

The hour of sunset varies very little, year-round, about 7.30 p.m., with brief twilight.

11.6 Telephone

Think twice before phoning home from your hotel. Typical cost is £20 for a 3-minute minimum call to UK. Carefully check the rules. In theory, the computer system shouldn't start counting your time until you get a response from the number you are dialling. But some hotels advise that you shouldn't let the phone make more than five rings. Otherwise a minimum 3-minute charge is automatically charged to your account.

Some hotels charge you in three-minute bites. So, if you talk for 3 minutes 5 seconds, you are billed for six minutes. Most hotels require a deposit, such as £40, before putting you through. Nowhere in the Dominican Republic can you make a reverse charge phone call.

There is a less expensive alternative. All the main towns have a CODETEL Centro de Telecomunicaciones, where a 3-minute call to UK would cost about £8. If you talk fast, you could even get by with a one-minute minimum charge; or you could send a fax. CODETEL is a virtual private-sector monopoly, but a less expensive company called TRICOM is beginning to make inroads, and also charges even cheaper rates at weekends. Another new company is called ALL AMERICAN, and likewise offers lower prices.

To call Britain dial (44) for UK, omit the zero of the STD code and continue to dial as normal. Don't forget the 5-hour time difference.

To call a Dominican Republic number from abroad, dial (010)-1-809- followed by the 7-digit local number.

Where to find telephone centres

Puerto Plata – Plaza Turisol
Sosúa – Alejo Martinez /corner Roberto Matos
Boca Chica – Plaza Boca Chica
Juan Dolio – Centro Comercial, Plaza Quisqueya
Playa Dorada – Cefumba Tours travel agency in Plaza Shopping Centre. They have a connection with TRICOM.

Incidentally, the postal service is extremely slow and unreliable. It can take six weeks for an air-mail card or letter to arrive. Columbus crossed the Atlantic faster in 1493. Mail addressed to the Dominican Republic is often mis-routed to the island of Dominica.

11.7 News

There are six local Spanish language morning newspapers and three afternoon dailies. The 'Santo Domingo News' and the 'Puerto Plata News' are English language weeklies that focus mainly on tourist events; 'Touring' is a multi-language tourist weekly; 'Hispaniola Business' is a monthly business and tourist paper in English.

Magazines and newspapers such as the 'Miami Herald', 'Wall Street Journal', 'International Herald Tribune',

'Financial Times' (US edition), 'Newsweek' and 'Time' are available a day or two after publication.

Television – Most hotel satellite TV's give you local Spanish-language programmes, news by courtesy of CNN, and other channels from America's deep south. The visitor from UK can feel very cut off from more important home news such as the cricket scores.

It's worth travelling with a short-wave radio, to pick up the regular on-the-hour news bulletins of the BBC World Service. Reception varies according to time and location, and can always be improved if you take a length of aerial wire to dangle from your hotel window. Try the following wavelengths:

Morning 7.00-10.00 hrs – 15220 kHz on 19-metre band; 6195 kHz on 49m band.

Day-time 10.00-12.15 hrs – 17840 kHz on 16m band.

Evening 18.00-00.30 hrs – 9915 kHz on 31-metre band; 7325 on 41m band; 5975 kHz on 49m band (from 16 hrs).

11.8 Security

The Dominican Republic is a low-risk country for holidaymakers and their valuables. A cautious policy is to put your credit cards, traveller cheques, jewellery, passport and return ticket into safe deposit boxes. Many hotels have a room safe at a small charge, and disclaim liability for any loss. But really the chance of theft is low, especially in the all-inclusive hotels which control entry at the perimeter gate.

Walking is comparatively safe. But late at night it is advisable to use a taxi and avoid carrying large sums of money.

A warning: unlike some other Caribbean islands, the Dominican Republic does not take a laid-back tolerant view on drugs. Jail sentences or fines are massive. If caught with even a tiny quantity of narcotics, it could cost several thousand dollars to get out of prison. Don't risk it!

11.9 Photo hints

In the brilliant Caribbean sunshine, slowish films around ASA 100 will give good results for colour prints. Concentrate your picture-making on early morning or late afternoon. Noontime sun makes people squint, and the strong light on beaches casts very harsh shadows. Also, the midday sun gives too much glare, though a lens hood and a polarization filter can help overcome the problem.

Towards evening, dusk is of short duration. Capture that sunset picture quickly, before it disappears! Make your beach photos more interesting with a foreground tree as a frame or silhouette.

Fine sand on the lens can be a nuisance. Keep the lens cap in place, whenever the camera is not in use. Bring some lens-cleaning tissue and a dust brush. To protect the lens, it's worth leaving a skylight filter permanently in place - much less costly to renew if over-vigorous cleaning causes scratches. Don't leave your camera lying in the sun, as heat can harm the film.

In the principal tourist locations, local people are accustomed to visiting shutterbugs with their desire to point cameras in every direction. Elsewhere, folk may be less tolerant of any invasion of their privacy.

However, if you don't make a big production of it, you can still get colourful shots of people in characteristic activity. Position yourself by a monument or in a crowded market, or at a crossroads. With a wide-angle lens for close-up, or long-focus lens for more distant shots, you can discreetly get all your local-colour pictures without irritating anyone.

Take flash for pictures of evening activities and entertainments – but photography in casinos is not allowed.

Film prices are elastic, depending where you buy. Generally they cost more than in Britain or USA, so take plenty. If you use a specialised film, rather than standard brands, then take an over-supply. Off-beat films are hard to find. Even the favourite international films may not be available when you run out.

Keep a note of photos taken, and their sequence. Otherwise, back home, it's very difficult to identify every picture. In postcard size, one beach can look remarkably like another.

Chapter Twelve

Further reference

12.1 Quick facts

Population: About 8,000,000. Annual rate of population growth – 2.3%. Multi-racial, multi-cultural society of Spanish background. White 16%, Negro 11%, Mixed 73%. Haitians are the largest minority group, over 1,000,000 mainly working on sugar plantations.

Religion: 95% Roman Catholic.

Life expectancy at birth: 63 years.

Education: Free and compulsory between 7 and 14 years of age. Children are taught in three shifts a day – morning, afternoon and evening. Almost 70% of the population is literate. The country has five universities, including the University of Santo Domingo (founded 1538), the oldest university in the Americas.

Constitution: The government is headed by a president and vice-president elected every four years by universal adult suffrage. President Joaquin Balaguer was elected to his sixth term in 1990, at age 83. National Congress comprises a 27-member senate and 120-member chamber of deputies. Members of both houses serve 4-year terms. An election is scheduled for 16 May 1994; inauguration on 16 August.

Administration: Is divided into 29 provinces and the capital district, each with its own civil governor.

Political parties: Major parties are the Reformist Social Christian Party (PRTC), Dominican Liberation Party (PLD), Dominican Revolutionary Party (PRD), Independent Revolutionary Party (PRI), and about 20 other active parties.

Major cities: The capital is Santo Domingo (de Guzman), the oldest and largest city in the Caribbean with a population of over 2.2 million. Santiago (de los Caballeros) is second with 500,000. La Romana 150,000; Puerto Plata 97,000; Higuey 84,000; Samaná 50,000; Sosúa 20,000.

National tree: Mahogany.

Military service: is not obligatory.

12.2 Festivals and holidays

Following the Catholic calendar, communities throughout the country celebrate the individual feast day of their local patron saint with festivals and folklore. To track them down, watch the local English-language press for details of where events are taking place.

Among the most popular are the feast of "Santa Cruz de Mayo", celebrated in the town of El Seibo each May; the "Ga-Ga", a mystical Easter week celebration in sugar cane villages (Bateyes); and the "Cachuas", typical of the southwestern town of Cabral, and held between Good Friday and Easter Monday.

Carnival erupts during February, and – contrary to worldwide custom – is not linked to Shrove Tuesday. Carnival parties and popular street fairs are held throughout the month, everywhere in the Republic, with devil-masked revellers prowling the streets in search of sinners.

The most important carnival celebrations are held in La Vega, where the colourful "Diablos Cojuelos" are out every Sunday afternoon during February. In Santiago, the city that best preserves the country's carnival traditions, the "Lechones" run free in a brilliant fiesta. In Montecristi there are "Bulls and Civilians"; in San Pedro de Macorís, the "Guloyas"; while "Diablos Cojuelos" roam the rest of the country. Each region features distinctive handcrafted masks.

The big climax is a colourful parade on February 27 – the Dominican Republic's Independence Day – along the Malecón promenade (George Washington Avenue) in Santo Domingo. A procession of extravagant costumes and decorated floats ends in a wild open-air party with dancing, drinking and eating. It's also a red-letter day for pickpockets. Parallel parades are held throughout the country. If you cannot see Carnival live, watch the local TV coverage. There's a repeat performance on August 16, to mark the founding of the Dominican Republic.

Heineken Jazz Festival draws top international jazz artists every March to Altos de Chavón, La Romana.

Merengue Festival is held in Santo Domingo from the last week of July to the first week in August, to mark the anniversary of the founding of Santo Domingo on August 4th. Bands perform the country's national music at major hotels and on the Malecón. A similar Festival is held in Puerto Plata during the last two weeks of October. Both events include street fairs, parades, handicraft fairs, Creole-cuisine gastronomy and fast food.

Christmas celebrations begin early December and finish with Epiphany Day on January 6 – a public holiday – when children finally get their Christmas gifts.

Public holidays

Stores, banks and most businesses close on:

January 1, New Year's Day
January 6, Epiphany Day
January 21, Our Lady of Altagracia Day
January 26, Juan Pablo Duarte's Birthday
February 27, Independence Day
Good Friday, variable
May 1, Labor Day
Corpus Christi Day, variable
August 16, Dominican Restoration Day
September 24, Our Lady of Mercedes Day
October 12, Columbus Day
December 25, Christmas Day

12.3 Useful addresses

There is no tourist office in the UK. For further information on the Dominican Republic send a self-addressed A4 envelope to the address below, together with 50p in stamps.

Honorary Consulate of the Dominican Republic,
6 Queens Mansions,
Brook Green,
London W6 7EB.
Tel: (071) 602 1885. Open 10-13 hrs Mon-Fri.

Dominican Tourist Office Information Center,
485 Madison Avenue,
New York,
NY 10022.

Tourism Promotion Council,
Desiderio Arias No. 24,
Bella Vista,
Santo Domingo,
Dominican Republic.
Tel: 0101-809-535-3276; FAX: 535-7767

Dominican Republic Ministry of Tourism,
George Washington Ave.,
Presidente Vicani Corner,
Santo Domingo 497,
Dominican Republic.
FAX: (1-809)-682 3806